ISBN 978-1-331-21327-7
PIBN 10159179

FB &c Ltd, Dalton House, 60 Windsor Avenue, London, SW19 2RR.
Company number 08720141. Registered in England and Wales.

For support please visit www.forgottenbooks.com

The relations between poetry, history, philosophy and theology

KILMAHOE

A HIGHLAND PASTORAL

With other Poems

BY

JOHN CAMPBELL SHAIRP.

London and Cambridge
MACMILLAN AND CO.
1864.

EDINBURGH: T. CONSTABLE,

PRINTER TO THE QUEEN, AND TO THE UNIVERSITY

TO MY FATHER

THIS POEM

INTENDED TO ILLUSTRATE A MANNER OF LIFE

WHICH PREVAILED IN THE LOWER HIGHLANDS

DURING HIS YOUTH

BUT HAS NOW PASSED AWAY

IS DUTIFULLY AND AFFECTIONATELY INSCRIBED.

CONTENTS.

KILMAHOE—

FROM THE HIGHLANDS—

FROM THE BORDERS—

KILMAHOE.

KILMAHOE.

I.

THE OLD LAIRD.

Upon a ledge of hillside lea,
'Mid native woods the white house peeps
Down one green field upon the sea,
And o'er the sea to Arran steeps.
In front far out broad reaches smile
Of blue sea, flanked on either hand,
Here by a porphyry-columned isle,
There by a forward brow of land.
No day nor season but doth wear
Some grandeur or some beauty there;
Spring with its song-birds all alive
  Through the copses and mountain leas,
While Ailsa every morn doth hive
With gull and gannet to swim or dive
  That sheen of sunny seas.
And though summer-time from sea and hill
May many a rainy day distil,

Yet when sunshine comes, it comes so bright,
Each breath you draw is a new delight;
One day of that transparent air
Is worth a hundred days elsewhere.
But, bright or dark, from year to year,
All seasons, happy or austere,
That home behind its hillside lawn,
Among its bielding woods, withdrawn
Apart, with this secluded shore
Wholly to itself made o'er,
Hears, night and day, the murmurous lave
Of the flowing and backgoing wave,
Up the burn-hollows borne, combine
Soothingly with the sughing pine,
Blend with the shimmering summer leaves
Around the swallow-haunted eaves,
And make through the lone glens the sound
Of all their torrents more profound
And slumberous, as from mountains thrown,
They plunge to presence of a moan
More everlasting than their own.
Ay! fair the place, but not less fair
Young faces, lightsome forms, are there,
Yea, a whole family life complete,
Embosomed in that lown retreat,
Loud with blithe voices, bright with looks
Of children, native to the clime,
As minnows to the mountain brooks,
Or to the summer braes the thyme.

But to fairest faces and loveliest home
Dark days, though long delayed, will come;
And at Kilmahoe, now the summer gone,
And golden autumn grown chill and wan,
To-day the cloudy November wind
Comes moaning down the hills behind,
Through the corrie glens and the copses sere,
The birk and the rowan tree,
Whirling the last leaves of the year
Down to the wintry sea.

But though November blow lorn and grey,
In quiet here falls the Sabbath-day:
The family all to the kirk have gone,
Some by the hill-path, some by the shore,
And little Moira left alone,
Is tending her father within the door,
His own little lassie well pleased to stay
With her ailing father this Sabbath-day.

Long time hath the Laird been dwining;
His day is down the vale declining;
He goes not now to his week-day work,
Empty his seat in the parish kirk.
For forty years that life hath been
Like a long summer day serene;
With cares indeed, that come to all,
Grave cares, yet broken in their fall,
By a soul that takes with meek content
What good or evil God hath sent.

And yet his earliest manhood cast
'Mid Scotland's mournfullest wars and last,
Had heard that wild war-welcome ring
To Athole braes from Knoidart—
My king has come, my own true king,
Has come ashore at Moidart!
And when the tidings southward came,
That Highland bosoms all aflame,
Glengarry, Keppoch, loved Lochiel,
To their true prince, for woe or weal,
Were plighting troth, and thronging round
His standard reared on Scottish ground—
Glenfinnan by the lone Loch-Shiel;—
Then for King George rose great Argyll,
His Campbells summoned from strath and isle,
And the Laird, true to clanship's laws,
His chieftain followed, not the cause.

Oft told he how i' the Forty-five,
A youth, he saw the western clans,
Clanranald and Glengarry, drive
From Corryarrick mountain down
On lowland village farm and town;
And flying 'mid the red-coat rout
Heard, not unpleased, the conquerors shout
Their slogan over Prestonpans.
Again he saw, that other day,
As fierce a charge, more wild deray,
When the clans burst on front and flanks,
With bared cla mores and hideous yell.

And the astonied red-coat ranks,
Like grass before the mowers, fell,
Or flying far and near like stour,
Driven before the strong west wind,
Left many a brave heart cold behind
The auld faile-dykes on Fa'kirk muir.

That day of dool, he was not thère
On dire Culloden,—did not share
The horror of that sickening sight,
The carnage and the murderous flight.
Enough he saw of ruthless wrong
While for his chief he held Kilchurn,
And watched the unleashed trooper throng
Let loose to slaughter and to burn.
Many a night of mute despair
Saw he the welkin lurid red
With the death-fires' baleful glare,
From Badenoch o'er Lochaber spread
Far west to Ardnamurchan head;
And heard dim voices of lament
From the far off mountains sent,
Homeless wives and famished bairns,
Crying 'mid the misty cairns,
For their sires that slaughtered lay
By the smouldering sheilings far away.
Much pitied him, their rueful plight;
He tendered all of help he might,
And men believed his heart the while
Was more with Charlie than Argyll.

With that, his day of warfare o'er,
Was sheathed for ever his claymore,
And long have these wild scenes been tales
To tell beside the red peat-fire,
When the scant winter daylight fails,
And the bairns gather round their sire.

Much from the outer world apart
He lived, a man of other heart
From those rough lairds on either shore
Of long Kintyre, whose wild delights
Were most to bury days and nights
In the wassail and the splore.
When some ship, with contraband
Freighting, hove in sight of land,
Like eagles scenting on the gale
Some fresh quarry, they her sail
Far-kenning, to the house repaired
Of the nearest brother laird,
Broached her casks, whate'er they be,
Bordeaux, or rarer malvoisie,
And sat from noon to noon at dine,
Spicing with high oaths their wine,
Each pledging each, with clenchèd hands.
Till broken health and deep-dipped lands,
All too early made it good—
That rude bond of brotherhood.

Meek man, removed alike from strife

And riot, flowed his stream of life;
Each morning, these forty years and more,
He hath been stirring by crow of cock,
When dark, at business within the door,
In summer, with workers on fallow or lea,
Down on the home-fields by the sea,
Or up to the hill among the flock.
At noon he walked to his farmer folk,
O'erlooked their crofts, of their matters spoke,
And with a kindly or warning word
The lagging and the down-hearted stirred.
Cottars and fishermen, far and near,
Dwellers on either side Kintyre,
Flocked hither for justice or help in need,
He heard and gave their heart's desire;
And few were they from that home would go,
But blessing the Laird of Kilmahoe.
Afternoon in the garden found him
With the bairnies playing round him
Or guiding them to some hidden nook,
Where the fairy well distils
Amid the many-folded hills,
Or up high summits that forth look
On gleaming seas beyond long defiles,
Where the sun goeth down to the outmost isles,
That flame with his glory and lap him away
To western worlds and the new-born day.
Then homeward down the hillside pacing,
Would they meet the moon their pathway facing,

Just as, from Arran peaks set free,
She rose full-orbed o'er the land-locked sea,
Through blue sky and marlèd cloud to go
Onward to quiet Kilmahoe,
And rain down there through her pearly fleece
On the window panes meek light of peace.

And every week as the Sabbath fell,
And the hills re-echoed the old kirk bell,
Winter and summer that reverent face
Was seen of all in the well-known place,
A beautiful life! but nearly o'er:
To market or kirk he'll return no more.

But since he must at home remain,
Little daughters he hath twain,
Gentle lasses, that love to stay,
Each the alternate Sabbath-day,
And tend their father. Their fond eyes
Meet all his wants before they rise,
And make old age and its weakness be
Sweet for their loving ministry.
They move about him, sister peers,
Albeit diverse in soul and mien,
One year between them, both their years
The tender side their earliest teen.
The elder Moira, nature's child,
Wild grace about her being shed
From lone shore, and far mountain head,

Yet with home sweetness reconciled.
Adown her shoulders fell rich flow
Of clusters auburn with the glow
Of the warm Highland summers in them ;
And cheeks, that, flushed with young light, win them
Love from all who look thereon;
Eyes that under white brows shone,
Quiet wells of light, till came
Into their orbs a finer flame,
As feeling wrought, and flushed them through
With its soft inner violet hue.
And in her voice would go and come
An under cadence, soft as chimes
Of bees abroad on the heather bloom,
Or murmuring from the flowering limes.
And Marion, flaxen haired and shy,
With less of beauty, and an eye
Meek and trembling as a dove's,
That looks and longs for that it loves,
And finds it in the sister dear,
Her elder, yet her perfect peer,
A playmate, yet a strength above her,
For her to love, and eke to love her.

This drear November Sabbath-day
Is Moira's turn at home to stay,
And while the rest by the sea-shore road,
Or the hill-path wend to the house of God,

Soon as the last from sight are gone,
And the laird and his daughter left alone
In the room that o'er the sea doth look,
He laid on the table the Holy Book,
And showed her the chapter and psalms wherein
He would have her read. They spake of sin,
By man deep-felt, by God forgiven,
And joy over penitent souls in heaven;
Of the wandered sheep from the mountains bare
Won back by the good Shepherd's care.
Of the Father's heart that doth wait and yearn
To welcome the lost son's return;
Of patience, faith, and love's increase,
That deepen into endless peace.
As she sat and read at her father's feet,
Her Highland voice fell soothing sweet,
As the cushie's croon in the autumn noon,
'Mid the gloom of beechen trees;
Or the burn from the hill in the gloamin' still,
Down-falling to moonlight seas.
It ceased, that voice,—her father said,
'Earth hath no words like these.'

He rose, and with him his little child,
Forth to the air so moist and mild;
But they turn not now to their wonted walks,
Where the garden rots with its blackened stalks,
And flowers are blanched or sere.

And only the pensive mignonette
A last faint beautiful regret
  Breathes on the dying year.
Under the dripping copse they went
  From the old mansion door,
Hand in hand down the smooth descent
  By the greenwood path to the shore.
The tide was past the full noon-flow,
And the ebb begun an hour ago,
Rasping with long back-swinging reach
The shingly stones down the mounded beach.
Among the rocks lay many a pool
Of sea-weed and crawling creatures full;
A hern stood dosing, here and there,
On the great black rocks left dripping bare;
Onward the base of Auchnahaun
For ever chafed by the billows wan,
While round its forehead in ceaseless wail
The clamorous gulls with the gannet sail.

He walks and heeds not the busy surge
  Murmuring at his feet,
His eye is afar on the misty verge,
  Where sky and ocean meet,—
Not on a sunny sail in sight,
But yon sudden shaft of sheer sunlight
  Hath parted the clouds and let in the sky,—
  It is that absorbs him, soul and eye.
Sometimes the child would saunter, beguiled

By shells on the sea marge strown,
Or coral shreds, from their oozy beds
By the latest tempest thrown.
Sometimes she bounded on before,
Leaping and singing for glee,
As the happy chime of her heart kept time
With the white waves far to sea,
And her hair, sunny brown, went a-wandering down
Her shoulders unconfined,
And ever as she played, it gleamed and swayed
In the waff of the westlin wind.
And her young cheek glows like the wild June rose,
Or the sheen from the hillside shed,
When the morning light some heathery height
Kindleth to purple red.
Sometimes she his hand would take,
And beside him walk,
But small answer he would make
To her innocent talk.
Only now and then he smiled
From out grave thoughts upon his child.
She was aware, but knew not why,
It was not with him as in days gone by:
That gleesome lass, how could she know
What cause had made the natural flow
Of his old spirit so faint and low?
In silence she walked a little space,
Then upward gazed on her father's face:

'Yonder the clouds come loaded with rain.
Father, we'll turn to our home again.'
By a different path they reached the door,
And he will return to that beach no more;
And she will remember when far away,
And far years on, when her hairs are grey,
  The hours with her father spent to-day.

II.

THE HOUSEHOLD.

This bleak March morning bitterly
The east wind shears from Arran o'er,
And even the low fields by the sea
Are white with cranreuch hoar.

But here—a grey plaid round her thrown,—
Comes staff in hand, through frosty rime,
To see, the lady widow lone,
Her ploughs a-yoke in time.

And with her Marion, early awake,
Intent her mother's rounds to share,
While yonder, breathless to o'ertake
These slipt forth unaware,

Comes Moira racing down the brae,
The same who with her father dear,
By the sea walked, that Sabbath-day,
In the fall o' the year.

Why through the March wind's bitter blow,
Ere the sun 's up, are these astir,
Young creatures? errands, to and fro
They gladly run for her,

Keep warm their blood ;—and doubtless she,
  Their mother, feels their sunshine dart
Some gleam of its own native glee
  To her care-clouded heart.

There on the headrig's unploughed grass.
  Awhile all three, they take their stand,
While up and down the two ploughs pass
  Turning the green lea-land.

Then to the shore, to see how speed
  The women-workers sent to save
The stranded wrack, or floating weed,
  That rocks i' the hungry wave.

" Now hain it weel, we'll wale the best
  To make these lands, they 're ploughing, yield
A richer harvest, and the rest
  We'll spread o'er yon bare field."

Then up the hill, they look how fare
  The kylies cowering 'neath the brae,
And with them taits o' fodder bear,
  The late-won mountain hay.

So all day long from shore to hill,
  From hill through dairy, barn, and byre,
She journeys on with eident will,
  Nor once doth stop nor tire,

Beat summer sun, blow wintry drift,
The frugal lady, gently-born,
Plying her old-world Highland thrift,
Late e'en and early morn.

To ease her toil, two daughters take
Some household o'ersight, hour by hour,
And learn white barley scones to bake,
And knead the fine wheat flour.

The eldest, in her latest teen,
Gives learning to that younger pair,
Moira and Marion; morn and e'en,
These are her constant care.

For them, too, summer-time will yield
Such work as suits their little skill,
To ted the hay in new-mown field,
Or drive the ewes a-hill.

While one, the youngest, little lass,
Is playing round her nurse's knee:
Fair day or dark, no cloud may pass
Over that bairnie's glee.

But winter nights, not less than days,
Have mingled tasks and mirth in store,
When, daylight done, to the ingle blaze
All flock within the door.

In parlour ben the lady sits,
  A-birlin' at her spinnin' wheel,
And one sews, one the stocking knits,
  And learns to turn the heel;

While but the house,—as outside beats
  The rainy night's loud roaring din,
And the hearthstone happ'd with glowing peats
  Makes ruddy all within,—

Comes on the blithesome spinning hour,
  When, all the heavy day's darg done,
The maidens on the sanded floor
  Their wheels range, one by one;

And, this with big wheel, that with sma',
  The other with the twirling rock,
To the wool-task assigned them fa',
  Wool shorn from last year's flock.

Then lilting, blent with rock and reel,
  Goes ben the house, a heartsome hum.
Till Moira first, then Marion steal
  Away, full fain to come,

And listen, where the old world tale,
  By Murlie told, the night beguiles,
Or some dim Ossianic wail
  From the outer isles.

Or some weird sight will Flora tell,
By witches wrought off the grim Moil;
Or how the boar by Diarmid fell
In the Forest of Sli-Gaoil.

At times the shepherd's pipes would set
The young folk dancing to their clang,
Till overhead the glossy jet
Of the roof-rafters rang.

But ere night close, in parlour ben
For worship all the household meet,
And elder eyes would wander then
To one now empty seat.

They miss his mirth at evening meal,
His stories from the fireside chair,
But most, when the whole family kneel,
His earnest voice in prayer.

Far away and safe, within the veil
He rests; no need for him to pray;
But much for them, those dear ones frail,
Not safe, though far away;

The brothers three, but lately gone
From warm love and their old abode,
As best they may, to shoulder on
In the world's rough high-road.

Ah! sisters' hearts are altars where
Love of the distant and the dead,

In silent thought, or pleading prayer,
Burns on, a pure flame fed,

Yea! blending with their faith in God.
Self to consume, and earthly will,
Hallowing each spot, the dear ones trode.
Of glen, or shore, or hill.

This made their labours pleasant, made
All cares and self-denials sweet;
They would be countlessly repaid
If they once more might meet

Their brothers 'neath the old roof-tree,
And these hereditary lands
Pass down from all encumbrance free,
Into the elder's hands.

And so though come of good degree,—
Brave warrior chiefs of honoured name—
At many a household ministry
They worked, and thought no shame.

As pastors, later forebears strove,
In days of Scotland's darkest ills,
To feed the remnant, tyrants drove
To refuge 'mid these hills.

Long buried looks shine forth once more
From younger eyes; in these some trace
Old men descried of chiefs of yore,
More of the pastor's grace.

Yet they, though born of gentle blood,
  Grew not less gentle, but more true,
Because they nature's work-day mood,
  Even as her festal knew.

But while with patient thrift they hained
  The winter long their scanty store,
It marvel was, how much remained
  For neighbour kindness o'er.

When the best strawberries came in prime,
  Or golden-fruited autumn filled
The baskets, or at Martinmas time,
  When the mairt cow was killed

And salted for the winter meat;
  And hill-fed beef, and elder wine,
With puddings many, white and sweet,
  And other dainties fine

Were rife, they turned not west nor east
  To their rich neighbours, lord or laird,
But summoned to partake their feast,
  Some who but poorly fared.

"Now, Annie lass, ye'll rise and ride
  To-morrow morn," would the lady say,
"Where Donald's widow dwells beside
  The Machrahanish bay.

"And bid her come, the bairns and a',
  To see them here he aye lo'ed weel;
And coming back, ye'll stop and ca',
  And bid gude Auntie Nell."

In a rough cart, o'er rougher road,
  Up hill and down, well pleased they go,
Across the country, a blithe load,
  To kindly Kilmahoe.

Aunt Nell has donn'd her tartan dress,
  The minister 's lent his naig to ride,
And braw and blait her niece Miss Bess,
  Comes walking by her side.

But ere they came to the white yett,
  Into the green field by the sea,
There, the first welcome that they met,
  Was Moira sure to be,

And with her Marion; hand in hand
  They lead their merry playmates home,
Then out their garden plots to see,
And on, through wood, o'er mountain lea,
  From morn till noonday roam.

But shepherd Colin, canty carle,
  Aye ready at the leddy's will,
In the grey dawn, with flint-locked barrel
  In hand, hath ta'en the hill.

There round about the heathery knowes,
His collie close behind, he creeps,
Where, cackling shy, the red cock-grouse
His jealous outlook keeps.

Or low 'mid corrie birks he springs
The heathgame, or from brackens brown;
And, sure of aim, from whirring wings
Thuds the strong blackcock down.

Or haply, if the season 's here,
He hies, with home-made gaud and line,
To Corven water, mossy clear,
Where, fresh-bathed from the brine,

The salmon comes with stalwart leap,
Cheerily dashing at the flies,
Or from dark pool 'gainst cataract steep
Now springs, now quiet lies.

There, after many a wary cast,
When steady eye, and patient hand,
Despite mad plungings, safe at last
Have stretched him on the strand.;

A little while with eager eyes,
He marks the silvery spangles shine,
Then in plaid-neuk home bears the prize,
To grace the board at dine.

III.

THE ISLAND.

Off from the mainland, neither near nor far,
Not in the sea-view fronting Kilmahoe,
But northward to the left a mile or so,
Tower the bold porphyry cliffs of Isle Davar:
Linked to the land by a long sandy bar.
Whereon at ebb of tide a child may go
Dryshod to the island; but the returning flow
Quite cancels it, and though a herring yawl
For a brief space at the flood-tide may crawl
Gratingly over it, if, in haste to make
The harbour, some large craft the passage take,
She straight is stranded.

From that island's crown
Landward a slope of heather shelveth down
To meet the bar, but all the outer sides,
Sheer walls of porphyry, stem the swinging tides
The Atlantic sendeth, when the strong south-west,
Blowing his clarion, 'gainst the rock wall breast
Heaves the great billows.

On a breezy day
The island seen from hill-tops far away
Stands out encinctured white with zone of foam,
Like a fair maiden. View it nearer home,
Wave springs on wave against the adamant wall,
Leaping like lions, then to plash and fall
Down-driven, baffled, and to seethe and moan
Among the splintered blocks and boulders strown
Along the basement. Many a shuddering cry
Of seamen in their shipwrecked agony
Hath smote these cruel crags, in the blank dark
Of winter nights, when some poor helpless bark,
After long battle till the day grew blind,
Groping through night the harbour mouth to find,
Won for a haven but the iron-bound
Back of the island and the gulfs profound.
The top was grassy, but no shepherd housed
Nor fed flock there, only the wild goats browsed
O'er it, or lightly leapt from ledge to ledge,
Watching the sea surge o'er the dizzy edge.
All day that edge, gull-haunted and clanged-o'er,
Was loud with multitudinous uproar
Of gannet, kittiwake, and tern that wound,
A wheeling cloud, slow-eddying round and round,
With ocean minstrelsy that never fails,
But there from dawn to sunset wildly wails,
Shrill shrieks above, and countless wings of snow,
White-flashing breakers thundering far below.

Hither on a gentle day
O'er the tide-bare yellow sands
From Kilmahoe their happy way
Wends a threesome sister band.
Other two have gone elsewhere;
Little bairnie keeps at home;
Anne with these, her constant care,
Comes the island rocks to roam,
These her whole heart doated on
Moira fair and Marion.
Oer the line of tawny sand
Come the sisters hand in hand
Wandering on, with light steps springing,
Songs of very gladness flinging
On the blue and buoyant air,
Joyance borne from everywhere,
Thrilling through them unaware;
From the clear hills cast behind,
From the sea that heaves before them,
From the heavens by the north wind
Laid bare to their blue depths o'er them.
Sands o'erpast, beneath the rock
Round the base their way they keep,
Stepping on from block to block,
Between precipice and deep.

All along these jaggèd heights
Many are the wild delights,

Goats, that grass on scant ledge crop,
Or poise them on some skiey top;
Marten-cat, up smooth rock-face
Climbing to his crannied place;
Falcons paired, that wheel and wheel
High o'er splintered pinnacle;—
Sights to feed the children's eyes
With an ever new surprise.
Now they seaward gaze—for spring
Hath unloosed the gannet's wing,
And sent them to their hunting grounds
There to wheel unwearied rounds.
Sudden as a lightning flash,
Falling sheer, one cleaves the main;
One with heavy-pinioned plash
On the weltering surge again
Re-appears, and, flapping wings,
Gulps his prey, and skyward springs
Buoyant to his own domain.

"Ha! the tide is turning fast,
Yonder comes the ripple and foam,
Narrower, since at noon we pass'd,
Wanes the bar,—home, sisters! home."
Watchful, so spake sister Anne;
But the little ones lag behind,
Fain to linger, while they can.
Loath to leave, and turning oft,
As they saunter o'er the sand,

Not now flinging songs aloft,
Not carolling hand in hand.
Each alone, and pacing slow,
Far behind their sister go
The two younger, little heeding
Growing tide and shore receding.

The long lank Dorlin hath a mound
Heaped with shingle, large and round,
Angled, like an elbow joint,
Between the island and the point
Midway stationed ; there it bides,
Grating wear of wind and tides,
Changing shape and aspect still
At the fitful current's will.
When the tide is inward making
O'er all the Dorlin long it peers,
When it ebbs, these shores forsaking,
Soonest re-appears.

When they reach that mound i' the Dorlin,
Lo! what feast for children's eyes!
All its side that slopes to norlan'
Sprinkled with bright galaxies,
Many hued and shapèd shells,
As by hands of mermaids wrought,
Down in ocean's deepmost cells,
And by wild waves hither brought.
Faint blue some, as morning mist,

Some as flushed with sunset glow,
Violet some like amethyst,
Some pure white as new-fallen snow,
Or like foam on moonlight seas,
Frozen to fair forms like these.
Milky some, but like the gowans,
With their edges crimson-tipped,
Some like Autumn's ripest rowans,
All in blood-red colours dipped.
Richer wealth for children's hand
Never ocean laved to land.

As when a flight of goldspinks light,
Some wintry day on a thistly field,
Of wind and sleet they nothing weet,
Enamoured of the downy yield.
So, intent on this rare wealth,
They their little baskets piled
Unaware; till ocean's stealth
Hath the Dorlin quite in-isled.
Sudden starting, southward, nor'ward,
Anne looked forth,—on either hand
Gone the pathway,—back or forward,
They are quite cut off from land.
Not a moment now to waste,
In blind doubt, or blinder haste,
But with calm voice, undismayed,
" Sisters, be not ye afraid,
Yet ten minutes ere the tide

Can this Dorlin peak o'erride,
Ten full minutes, maybe longer,
Stay ye here, while I, the stronger,
Taller, wade the waters o'er,
And fetch Angus from the shore."

And with that, the gallant lass
Closelier wraps her plaidie round her,
And with fearless foot doth pass
In among the waves that bound her.
The very first step that she took,
She was wading to the knee—
Few steps farther—to the waist
She is plunging, wave-embraced,
Yet unfaltering on bears she.
By what strength her slender limb
Track or footing there could keep,
How she held, unused to swim,
Steady through that rushing sweep,
Nor was hurried to the deep,
No one knoweth. Not her own
Was the strength around her thrown,
Seem'd it that an unseen hand
Bore her to the shingly strand.

Albeit dripping, draggled dress
Leadlike round her limbs doth press,
Nought she feels, but, waving aloft
Wild hands, hurries to the croft.

"Angus, haste! my sisters save
From the jaws of the hungry wave,—
Yonder—on the Dorlin mound,"—
And with that, upon the ground
Sank outwearied.

They meanwhile
Prisoners on their vanishing isle,
Last speck of the sunken bank,
Frail as shipwrecked mariner's plank,
Their sister 'mid the drift of spray
Vanished quite—ah, well-a-day!
Lone lorn little ones, what do they?

The wind from point to point doth veer,
And, like a frantic charioteer,
Shouts to his wild steeds—proud, high-pacing,
White-manèd coursers, how they come!
From the deep o'er the ridge of the Dorlin racing,
To plunge and burst in thunder and foam.
Seaward one pale shuddering look,
Their faces dark 'gainst the 'blackening rook,'
One to the island, one to the shore,
Hapless children, look no more!
No hope from sea or land or air,
But Heaven 's above, there is pity there.
On the wet sands low they kneel,
To the heaven their meek appeal

Over the plash and the hoarse deep swell
Rises clear and audible,—
Moira's voice; but a sudden grey
Wild squall drives over them, blind with spray,
And near and nearer the waves are swaying,
Like a savage pack round their quarry baying.
And the spent wave's ooze begins to brim
Over the Dorlin's topmost rim,
Washing the two children's feet
In their inner last retreat.
Firm stood Moira, never a word,
But Marion, like a fluttering bird
Under the hawk, to her sister's breast,
Bitterly weeping, closelier prest.
"Dear Marion, hush!" but again the spray
Drives over and sweeps the words away,
And the oozy floor of the Dorlin-head
Sinks soft and unsteady beneath their tread,
And ocean and solid earth reel and swim
Around them in mists of anguish dim.

Just then an arm from out that cloud
Was reached, kind looks were o'er them bowed—
Strong kind looks of a long known friend,
Angus, the Fisher of Leear'side end.

Strong as life, tender as love,
One moment he stood the bairns above,

And the next, I wot, their hearts flashed high,
Up to the old man's loving eye,
I wot through every pulse and limb
Life throbbed back in the grasp of him.

He hath lifted Moira on his back,
And Marion 'neath his left arm braced,
And along the Dorlin track
Wadeth on in wary haste.
Stout his stride, and strong his will,
But the flood comes stronger still;
Deeper sinks the Dorlin road,
Heavier grows the living load;
Nothing now remains for him
But for life or death to swim.

Straightway plunging overhead,
Lost for ever, you had said.
But yonder see his form emerge,
Buoyant on the bounding surge,
One arm bearing up the child,
One against the rolling wild
Billows doing manly strife,
For his triple load of life.
This way, that way, long he swung
With the swinging surges, hung
Now on peakèd wave aloft,
Now in yawning furrow troughed,
Every nerve on tensest strain

Striving inch by inch to gain:
Wary eye, lest billow rolled
O'er them, may undo their hold.
Or benumb their grasp with cold;
Bravely straining, hardly gaining,—
Till one wave's benigner bound
Heaved him on to solid ground,
And against the setting sun.
All his vigour well-nigh done.
Bore he forth those children sweet.
And down laid his sea-drenched charge
At their death-pale sister's feet.
On the safe sea marge.
That one moment—only those
Who their loved have lost and found,
Can divine the rapturous close,
The strong heart's convulsive bound.
When, sea-peril overpast,
Their sister clasped them safe at last.

When they three arm-twining trode
Homeward by the shorelan' road.
The storm had past, and very still
Quiet was falling from sea to hill;
Single the gulls, or in scattered droves,
Wearily winged to the Leear'side coves,
And the evening star came out and shone
Serene o'er the headland of Auchnahaun.
All things were breathing a deep content,
As to their home these children went.

IV.

PAUL JONES.

THE time was wild, there did come o'er the sea a
troubled hum,
Of the marshalling of armies and of ships:
Kings from their thrones were dashed, and peoples,
madly clashed
Together, met in grim death-grips.

very hidden sluice of lawlessness was loose.
Evil men from restraint set free,
irates and brigands were hauntin lonely lands,
And prowling on every sea

hrough the grey summ ic sh
hath gone,
"Paul Jones comes s
nd startled mothers bi
And the manliest to

With the sou'-west l
night long
And the breakers
ow with flow of mo
He is setting for o

As from mountain-tops amain stoops the eagle to the plain,
See, with every stitch of sail unfurled.
He sweeps past Ailsa Craig with the sable pirate flag
Bearing death. from the western world.

Sheer on—he is bearing down on the little harbour town,
That crouched in its sheltered bay doth lie;
Will he try if the roof of Kilmahoe be proof
To his guns, as he sweepeth by?

Yet what [illegible] here? is his tackle out of gear.
Is he t[illegible] mast or yard?
What can [illegible] here only poor men live,
[illegible] this cr[illegible]

IV.

PAUL JONES.

The time was wild, there did come o'er the sea a
troubled hum,
Of the marshalling of armies and of ships;
Kings from their thrones were dashed, and peoples,
madly clashed
Together, met in grim death-grips.

Every hidden sluice of lawlessness was loose,
Evil men from restraint set free,
Pirates and brigands were haunting lonely lands,
And prowling on every sea.

Through the grey summer dawn up the shores the cry
hath gone,
"Paul Jones comes, yonder is his sail;"
And startled mothers prest their babies to their breast,
And the manliest cheeks turned to pale.

With the sou'-west blowing strong, he hath wrestled all
night long
And the breakers roaring white upon his lee,
Now with flow of morning tide from the Atlantic wide
He is setting for our inland sea.

Bearing fruit from the

IV.

PAUL JONES.

THE time was wild, there did come o'er the sea a troubled hum,
Of the marshalling of armies and of ships:
Kings from their thrones were dashed, and peoples, madly clashed
Together, met in grim death-grips.

Every hidden sluice of lawlessness was loose.
Evil men from restraint set free,
Pirates and brigands were haunting lonely lands.
And prowling on every sea.

Through the grey summer dawn up the shores the cry hath gone,
"Paul Jones comes, yonder is his sail;"
And startled mothers prest their babies to their breast,
And the manliest cheeks turned to pale.

With the sou'-west blowing strong, he hath wrestled all night long
And the breakers roaring white upon his lee,
Now with flow of morning tide from the Atlantic wide
He is setting for our inland sea.

As from mountain-tops amain stoops the eagle to the
plain,
See, with every stitch of sail unfurled,
He sweeps past Ailsa Craig with the sable pirate flag
Bearing death, from the western world.

Sheer on—he is bearing down on the little harbour
town,
That crouched in its sheltered bay doth lie;
Will he try if the roof of Kilmahoe be proof
To his guns, as he sweepeth by?

Yet what seeks he here? is his tackle out of gear?
Is he tempest-maimed, mast or yard?
What can our small port give, where only poor men live.
To fix this cruel man's regard?

Like men of reason reft, the fisher-folk have left
Their boats and their nets to the waves.
And are up wi' wives and bairns among the mountain
cairns,
The corries and dank dripping caves.

And all the harbour bay is tumult and deray,
Men and women hurrying here and there;
Some to cellars underground, and some have refuge
found,
High aloof on the uplands bare.

Yon veterans on the steep, by the ruined castle-keep,
With their rusty guns how crousely they craw!
"Let the pirate show his beak this side the island peak,
How his Yankee kaim we will claw!"

But at bonny Kilmahoe, will they stay? will they go?
What is doing at the old farm toun?
Men stand agape and stare, lasses skirl and rive their hair.
That's what they're doing, lass and loon.

But the lone lady fair, with braided silver hair,
Down has steppit, when she heard the din,
"Do ye think that ye will flout, wi' your senseless roar and rout,
Paul Jones from his entering in?"

"'Twere better, lads, belyve, that ye should rise and drive
The kye and calves to the burnie cleuch;
And lasses, screech na here, but haste and hide our gear,
In the house, atweel, there is wark eneuch."

Then up the stair she stept to where her bairnies slept
In an upper chamber ben,
"Now, Flory! haste thee, flee, wi' my bonnie bairnies three,
To the hills frae thae rover men.

There tide what may, they 'll be safe a' day
  I' the how o' the brackeny glen.'

Up the long broomy loan, wi' mickle dool and moan
  And out upon the hillside track,
Nurse Flory forward bent, crooning as she went,
  With the wee bairn clinging on her back.

But Moira hand in hand with Marion forward ran,
  Nor dool nor any care had they,
But they chased the heather bee, and they sang aloud for glee,
  As they hied up the mountain way.

When the hill-top they had clomb, one glance back to their home,
  And awesome was the sight that they saw;
Close in shore the pirate bark on the bright sea looming dark:
  On their little hearts fell fear and awe.

One quick glance at the ship, and o'er the edge they dip,
  And down to the long glen run;
Where the burnie gleams between its braes o' bracken green,
  And one lone sheiling reeks i' the sun.

There to daunder all the day, pu'ing bluewarts on the brae,
  Or the curls of the newly sprouted fern;

Or to Ailie's sheil out-owre, to bield them from the shower,
Or paidling barefoot in the burn.

But down at Kilmahoe all was hurrying to and fro,
And stowing away of the gear,
And the lady's self bare forth the things of choicest worth,
The heirlooms that her husband held dear.

And she dug for them a tomb beneath the snowy bloom
Of the old pear tree's hugest arm,
As tho' that giant of his race, the patriarch of the place,
By power of immemorial charm,
Girt the whole orchard ground with a magic safety round
And screened all within from harm.

"What can be done is done, weel ye've borne your part, each one:"—
To her elder daughters twain spake she,—
"Now ye maun climb outright to Crochnachaorach height,
And see what the end will be.
For me, I will abide my gude auld house beside,
While my house bides by me."

From that knowe in long suspense, with eager eyes intense,
They watch the dark hull heave to and fro,

As if through the harbour mouth, that opens on the south,
She would go, and yet would not go,
O'er her purpose pausing, like a falcon poised to strike,
Yet hovering ere he stoop below.

But the breeze sprung up off shore, and round the great ship wore,
With her head to the Atlantic main,
As the falcon down the wind sudden wheels, and far behind,
Leaves his quarry, to return no more again.

From many a hidden nook, from many a high outlook,
Straining eyes westward long were bent
On the dim tower of sail, with the evening fading pale,
Where the ocean with the heaven was blent.

Let them gaze, there is one cannot gaze till all be done,
She hath taken all unseen her way,
The lady, through the still of the twilight up the hill,
Where her heart hath been yearning all the day.

And there, out owre the knowes, hair streamed back from her brows,
And the mountain flush bright upon her cheek,
Came Moira, and her face plunged deep in that embrace—
And then Marion, too full at heart to speak.

Last of all, the lady prest her wee bairn to her breast.
And their hearts of joy had their fill;
As the covey to the call of moor-hen meets at fall
Of gloamin'. when the fowler leaves the hill.

Forth at morn they went and weeped, and joy at eve they reaped,
Yea. the day's pain, if tenfold more,
In the meeting of the night had found harvest of delight.
That repaid it o'er and o'er.

They who then were little ones, of the coming of Paul Jones.
And the fray of that affrighted morn,
Shall tell, as grey-haired dames, by yet unlit ingle flames.
To children that are yet to be born.

But what strange impulse bore to this secluded shore
That bark, none ever will make plain ;
Nor what sudden fear had sway to waft him west away
Back to night and the Atlantic main.

THE HIGHLAND FOX-HUNTER.

High up on the hill-tops the children are playing,
'Mid the moist clouds of April and fast flying gleams;
But, hark! thro' the mist comes a lone eerie baying.
As tho' grisly Bengollion were muttering in dreams.

Nay! start not, dear children, no hill-sprite appalling
Shrieks here—'tis the sleuth hound that bays on the track,
And there with the shepherds comes grey hunter Allan,
A-toiling since morn on the wake of his pack.

Far hence, where the last stars died down the Atlantic.
They hit on the drag of the wandering hill-fox.
And away to the mountains went knelling—till frantic
The baffled hounds bayed round his refuge of rocks.

Not long, they unearthed him, and this way come shaking
Carriedale and the deep Saddel-glen with their cry,
Where the clans 'mid grey ruins their long rest are taking,
And the lords of the islands stone-panoplied lie.

It hath burst on the silence of shepherds that follow
Their hirsels at noontide up high Ballochgaire;
Till Bengollion hath caught up the deep chime and hollo,
To startle the wandering bairns unaware.

Down by the Leear'side, die faint and fewer,
Voices of deep-throated hounds on the wind,
Pants Allan, sore-spent but unwearied pursuer,
With rough troop of terriers long miles behind.

Stay, gentle lasses! why strive with the stronger?
Not for you the wild chase and its headlong delight;
Well! if ye must, when tired limbs can no longer,
Watch from the hillside their far forward flight,

On by Dunaverty, time-rended ruin,
To the mid face of the sea-stemming Mull;
There let the hill-fox rest, safe from pursuing,
Under-boomed by the breakers, o'er-screamed by the gull.

At gloamin' returning, hounds weary and sullen,
Allan will shelter in warm Kilmahoe,
Sing battle chants of bard Oran and Ullin,
Tell the wild tales from the isles long ago.

VI.

THE GLEN.

In the glen by the shoreland
It is blithe to-day,
O'er ocean and o'er land
In flows the May:
Come, sisters, sweet sisters, with me!
The burn from the hillside is falling
Down the deep dell from linn to linn;
Merle and mavis aloud are calling
From the heart of the hazels within,
Come, children, to our green home!
And the cuckoo wandering from height to height
Thro' the hills is shouting his lone delight,
"Come, children, for Spring hath come."

Ay! mavis and merle are filling
All the glens with their lilting loud;
The burn, as it sings down its falls, distilling
O'er the brae-flowers a silvery cloud.
And the delicate birk-leaves are breaking
Into shimmer of sunny sheen;

Alder and rowan, and hazel awaking
To the life of the young leaves green
Then come, through the tangling of hazel and birk
We will track by her footprints of broider-work
The mazes where Spring hath been.

Come with me to the shy wood-places
With primroses all aglow,
From the shelves of the braes their starry faces
Were gleaming three weeks ago.
There anemones all a-quiver
In twilight of green leaves live,
Like delicate hearts, that tremble for ever.
To the rude world too sensitive.

And there the braes are all bracken-hung.
The queen-fern stately and rare.
The lady-fern and the long hart's tongue.
And the delicate maiden-hair.
And we'll wade knee-deep thro' the cool woodroof,
All white in its early prime,
And store its wood fragrance in willow-woof
'Gainst the flowerless winter time.
And we'll dive down the dells where the hyacinth bells
In the light winds are swinging blue.
And the sunlight, that slants down their lustrous haunts,
Is flushed to an azure hue.

And many a rare
Wee flower is there.
That did never in garden grow :
But all hidden nooks
Where their shy sweet looks
Are peeping forth. I know

So sang Moira—at her call
Forth they scramble, one and all.
Here and there, to climb and crawl
Up the braes at will:
Fain as lambs that run to meet
Their ewe-mothers' wistful bleat.
When, new-shorn, these set their feet
To their native hill :
In the many creviced glens.
That cleave deep the gnarled Bens.
Happy all-day denizens,
Of green mountain halls.
Far from women's eye and men's.
Startling roes from ferny dens.
Spying nests. where golden wrens.
In cool green moss-walls.
All the May-time hatch their young.
By budding hazels overhung.
Morn and midnight sweetly sung
To by sounding falls ;—
Watching the burn's many ways.
And its fairy fantasies,

Down the rocks, aneath the braes
How it wimples, jouks, and plays,
Now mute, now making din:
How amber light-flakes beautiful
Fall like leaves into the cool
Rock-o'ershadowed clear brown pool,
As to bask therein:
Till late meeting they unstore
Noonday meal on greensward floor
'Neath the oak, above the roar
Of the upper linn.

But ere day began to wane
Marion May took up the strain,
Flinging back her glad refrain:

I.

Come out to the hillside while sunset light
Down all the glens is streaming,
And the sound of the deep in his charmèd sleep
Comes up like a giant dreaming;
And the sun gone down beyond Kintyre,
West the Atlantic far in,
Is signalling back with his golden fire
To the splintered peaks of Arran.
Lo! each high peak answers with flushing flame,
All hues, red, green, and violet,
To the sunken sun whence their glory came,
High over firth and islet.

And yonder Ailsa lofty and lone,
  In the sunset brave and free,
Heaves his sheening sides, like a silver throne,
  From a floor of golden sea.
While far beyond, a pale outline,
The azure headlands of Galloway shine,
Like the dream-seen verge of a land divine.

II.

But when the light from crag to crown
  Fades upward, fainter, dimmer,
Hand in hand, we will wander down
  Where the wave-ripples glimmer.
With laughter and shout the rock-doves we will flout,
  Till flapping the loud cave-roof,
They 'scape overhead and their poised wings spread
  To the calm heavens aloof.

III.

Then when clouds come down
  On the mountain crest,
  And every bird
  In the glens is at rest,
Save one lone thrush singing
  Through the gloamin' still
To the folding star
  On the westlin hill,
  Weary yet cheery,

We will daunder home,
And tell mother dear,
Where we ranged and clomb,
And how blithe together
All day we have been,
By the shore, and the glen,
And the copse-wood green.

VII.

RANALD MACDONALD.

The Lammas tide was past, and harvest come,
With those bright days that empty every home,
And send the dwellers to the hills, away
To fetch the last peats or the mountain hay.
And every room in Kilmahoe is dumb,
Save when through open window the stray hum
Of hill-bee loiters, or from glooming beeches
The cushie's brooding croon a moment reaches
Into the hush, then leaves it as before.
But there are blithesome voices by the shore,
Mid the ripe corn; or 'neath the orchard trees,
With plump fruit laden; or on mountain leas,
Among the new-weaned lambs. But otherwhere
  Moira and Marion find delight to-day
Adown the Leear' side through the golden air,
  Sauntering and dreaming on their gladsome way.
For o'er their heads the heaven of softest blue,
Fleeced with white clouds, the moor all sheen with dew

Around them, lures their vagrant footsteps on
Toward the base of caverned Auchnahaun.
And on their way from plots of upland corn
Snatches of solitary singing borne
Come floating shoreward; then, in threes and fours,
Shy startled whaups fly screaming down the shores.
One while, they climb nooks nestled on the steep,
That all last spring-time smiled on the great deep
With tufts of bright primroses, but where now
Only the blue-bells in the west winds bow.
Another while, on hands and feet they crawl
Far ben the lesser caves, that, dark and small,
Scoop the grey promontory's rock sea-wall.
But one there was that more than all the rest
Had hither drawn their ever busy quest
Of new adventure. Ofttimes they had heard
Vaguely of Covie-Ciaran things that stirred
Their longings thither; now through that arched door
Inward they pass, all eager to explore
The many-hued moss-tapestries that drape
   The cave from roof to base; the ruined wall
That once had fenced it; and the rounded shape
   Of sculptured stone, with here and there a scrawl
On the rock sides, by nature wrought or man.
But farther in, where twilight dusk began
To grow to darkness, indistinct and dim
Before their senses all things melt and swim,
And creepings o'er them pass, an eerie fear
Of what they saw, or seemed to see and hear;

Till quite o'er-mastered both turn back and flee
Out to the daylight and the cheerful sea.
Still on, all afternoon from Auchnahaun,
By cove and sanded bay their steps are drawn
Down shores that wander endlessly away
Out to the isle-strewn illimitable main,
Till down its verge they've buried the bright day,
And wake to evening thoughts of home again.
So o'er the moor, a shorter shepherd's track
Behind the headlands, led them wearied back
Through heathery braes, and hollows sweet with gale.
Down to a burn where birks dew-drenched exhale
Their evening fragrance on the mountain air
Round Ranald's bothy, 'mid the copsewood there
Half hidden, with its own blue smoke of even,
Hung o'er it like a cloud let down from heaven.

Freely they enter, friendly comers they,
  Needing no bidding ere they lift the latch,
But welcomed readily with blithe good-day,
  Whene'er they pass beneath that heathery thatch.
'Come in, dear leddies, welcome!' Ranald said;
And the old man, hale-hearted, though his head
Was white with seventy winters, rose and came
Forward to greet them, with his gentle dame,
Old Evir Cameron. In her own she took
Their hands, and clasped them with a winning look
Of faithful love; for she inherited
The loyal heart, the courtesy inbred,

And manners sweet with that old Highland grace,
Born in the lowliest of the ancient race.
Inward they led the children to low seats,
Themselves had left before the glowing peats.
For they, just home returned from toilsome day,
Up in the hills at the late mountain hay,
Had lit a fire of peats and split bog-pine,
That from the stone-hearth sent a cheery shine.
Their daughter Una, with her long dark hair
Coiled o'er her sun-browned looks, moved here and there,
Preparing evening meal. The old folk sat
In the ingle nook, discoursing friendly chat
With the two little maidens, till at last
Young Marion, with a bright look upward cast,
'Ah Evir! wilt thou that sweet shealing strain,
You sang at last year's kirn, sing once again.'
It was a simple, yet a pleasing rhyme,
Breathed from far mountains and a fading time;
For Evir Cameron, her early days
And maiden summers were among the braes
Of high Lochaber. Donald met her then,
A blue-eyed lassie, in her native glen,
When the leal Stuart hearts were all alive
With their last hopes in gallant Forty-five.
But Evir to her daughter, 'Sing it thou;
Better than mine it suits thy youthful tongue;
Then Una stood erect with lifted brow,
And rafter-high the wild sweet music flung.

THE SHEALING SONG.

When the cry of the cuckoo is heard from the craig,
Then the milk on the kye will be flowing,
And we'll leave low Glen Spean, and up to Loch Treig,
And his bonny green shealings be going.

On the birk comes the leaf at the glad cuckoo cry,
And green braird to upland and hollow,
Comes bloom to the hillside, and warmth to the sky,
And to the still lochan the swallow.

Then we'll gae and theek owre wi' fresh heather and fern
The auld bothies a' simmer to be in,
Wi' our kinsfolk and neebors, by edge of the burn,
That sings doun the lone Corrie-veean.

And we'll toil at the cheese and the butter sae fine,
By the hill-flowers made fragrant and yellow,
While the bare-footed bairnies in pleasant sunshine
Will be pu'ing the blaeberries mellow.

O the bonny Craiguanach's ledges sae green!
It's the bonniest hill i' the Hielans,
As its green rocky shelves i' the sunset are seen,
Gleaming o'er the calm loch, frae the shealings.

And there, when the gloamin fa's lonesome and lown,
Unseen the wild Stag will be belling,
While louder the voice from its dark hollow down
Of Alt-coirie-essan is swelling.

Then Donald, from ranging by balloch and ben,
Where the mists and the ptarmigan hover,
Comes driving the milking goats doun to the pen,
Where Morag is waiting her lover.

And they sing, as she milks, and when milking is o'er,
Lang and late on the braeside they'll daunder,
And laith bid good-night at her ain bothy door,
Ilka day growing fonder and fonder.

But lang ere the hairst with its yellowin' corn
Ca's us doun to our hames by the river,
Will Donald and Morag the sure word have sworn,
That makes their twa hearts ane for ever.

"Ay, these were happy summers," Ranald said,
"But they, with those who lived them, all are dead:
Come sing yoursel' the clearance song; I trow,
It better suits the Highlands, that are now."

CLEARANCE SONG.

From Lochourn to Glenfinnan the grey mountains ranging,
Naught falls on the eye but the changed and the changing,
From the hut by the lochside, the farm by the river,
Macdonalds and Cameron pass—and for ever.

The flocks of one stranger the long glens are roaming,
Where a hundred bien homesteads smoked bonny at gloaming,

Our wee crofts run wild wi' the bracken and heather,
And our gables stand ruinous, bare to the weather.

To the green mountain shealings went up in old summers
From farm-toun and clachan how mony blithe comers!
Though green the hill pastures lie, cloudless the heaven,
No milker is singing there, morning or even.

Where high Mam-clach-ard by the ballach is breasted,
Ye may see the grey cairns where old funerals rested,
They who built them have long in their green graves been sleeping,
And their sons gone to exile, or willing or weeping.

The Chiefs, whom for ages our claymores defended,
Whom landless and exiled our fathers befriended,
From their homes drive their clansmen, when famine is sorest,
Cast out to make room for the deer of the forest.

Yet on far fields of fame, when the red ranks were reeling,
Who prest to the van like the men from the shealing?
Ye were fain in your need Highland broadswords to borrow,
Where, where are they now, should the foe come to-morrow?

Alas for the day of the mournful Culloden!
The clans from that hour down to dust have been trodden,
They were leal to their Prince, when red wrath was pursuing,
And have reaped in return, but oppression and ruin.

It's plaintive in harvest, when lambs are a-spaining,
To hear the hills loud with ewe-mothers complaining—
Ah! sadder that cry comes from mainland and islands,
The sons of the Gael have no home in the Highlands.

And as old Evir's voice, that trembling rose,
Went wailing downward to its slow, sad close,
Low Ranald sighed, "Owre true, owre true the tale,
The Lairds are set on sheep, muir-game, and deer,
And care na' that their ain true-hearted Gael
From the old mountains vanish year by year."

But Moira quickly turning from the stress
Of thoughts too sad for her young happiness,
"Come, Ranald, tell us what of yore befell
That hath so long made Covie-Ciaran's cell
An awesome place; then travelling down unfold
All this land's story from the days of old."

Ranald Macdonald, none knew more than he,
The blended lore of bard and seannachie,
A far descended, though a lowly man,—
One of few remnants of the elder clan,
That in Kintyre before the Campbells ruled,—
His heart, from earliest childhood, had been schooled
In old tradition; through his soul had rung
The wild war-music of the songs that strung
Men's hearts to die for the old kingly line;
And when their standard, ere their last decline,
O'er Moidart mountains, like a sunburst, shone,
And all Clan-donald by the strong spell drawn
Were thronging round their Prince, with his brave sire,
Young Ranald went,—they only from Kintyre,—

To meet the gathering clans. Though scarce sixteen,
Many a stirring, many a piteous scene
Of that stern time he shared. The wild delight
Of charge and victory—then disastrous flight.

And when the conquerors' fires from all the glens
Sent up their savage smoke, they flying clomb,
He and his father, to the loftiest Bens,
And made the mists their ever shifting home.
There, moving with the clouds, beside the clear
High mountain wells they watched the straggling deer,
To strike them down for food. So by distress
And hunger taught, young Ranald soon became
Quick-eyed to sight far off the antlered game,
Haunter unwearied of the wilderness,
Known for the hardiest stalker, and the best
Of aim, through all the mountains of the west.
And many ventures more, on midnight hill
With trusty friends he tried in hidden cave,
Streaming the barley bree from secret still,
Ere yet the Gael had learnt to think it ill,
Though man forbade, to use what nature gave.
And then in boats with freighting contraband,
What hairbreadth 'scapes he had; what crafty wiles
On the main shore he plied; or through the isles;
Before the King's ships scudding, to make land,
And plunge to unknown caverns, where great seas
Wash the gnarl'd headlands of the Hebrides.
In such strange life gleaned Ranald ample store

Of Celtic legend, song, and antique lore,
Enough to furnish tales for every night,
The whole long winter by the peat-fire's light.
At last tired out, now many years ago,
  With homeless wandering, he returned and found,
Under the kindly laird of Kilmahoe,
  Safe shelter, and a farm of mountain ground,
Where he and Evir might have peace and food,
Near his own birthplace, for their little brood,—
Five blue-eyed bairns. There 'mid his healthful toil.
The good laird's kindly influence fell like oil
Of healing on his spirit; to subdue
What there was harsh or wild, and open new.
Or long unheeded springs of deeper truth,
That had lain buried 'neath his stormy youth.
And now, this life receding, and more near
  The confines drawing of the life beyond,
Still voices thence more clearly reached his ear,
  More fully learnt his spirit to respond.
For him old things had nearly passed away;
  Yet in his house one relic still was laid
  On the smoked rafters, the Ferrara blade
His father bore on dark Culloden day.
At sight whereof sometimes the past would gush
  Back on his soul, and loose the full rich stream
Of speech, till his wan cheek recaught the flush
  Of youth, his weird grey eye its fiery gleam.
Yet ever as the feuds of clan with clan
  And the old battles he recounted o'er,

Through all his words an undertone there ran,
  The heart-deep echo of a holier lore,
That blended with his chaunt, as forth he rolled
These gathered memories of the great of old.

VIII.

RANALD'S TALE, OR OLD KINTYRE.

O Covie-Ciaran's a bonny cave,
As ever rock-doo haunted!
And there for ages wind and wave
Their orisons have chaunted.
But holier than the cooing bird,
Or sounds from air and ocean,
A saintly voice that cave once heard,
Upraised in rapt devotion.
Those echoes from the roof have ceased,
A thousand years and more,
But still the cave door fronts the east,
Unspread, the table, fast or feast,
Lies bare upon the floor—
That rounded stone with strange unknown
Characters sculptured o'er;
Springs dimpled still the clear rock well
With roof-drops falling, as they fell
In the dim days of yore.
The hands that shaped them are at rest
Long since, the good Culdee is blest;

His name on earth hath long gone dim,
But I'll tell thee all I've heard of him.

II.

Of old when sons of Erie borne
  In coracles came wafted o'er
From Erin,—Angus, Fergus, Lorn,—
  To land on this lone shore,
Here these Dalriad chiefs became
The builders of our Scottish name;
This was their earliest dwelling-place,
The sires of Scotland's kingly race.
Rude were they then, a warlike clan,
  Intent on battle, chase, and spoil;
But soon there came a saintly man
  Bowed down with holier toil.
He had been reared in Erin while
Saints owned her for their nursing isle;
But his heart went forth in pity and ruth
  For them, his wandering kinsmen, gone
To lands where yet no light of truth
  Through the thick darkness shone.
He came and made that cave his home;
Its doorway, by the seething foam
Twice daily laved, beholds the streaks
Of morning behind Arran peaks
Long-drawn. Thence going far and near,
He travelled to impress the fear

Of God on men who knew it not,
Or knowing had almost forgot.

III.

Oft when a pause upon the din
Of battle fell, a voice of peace,
He pled with men grown grey in sin
From ruthless deeds to cease.
Toil-wearied to his rocky lair
'Neath the bleak headland he withdrew,
By days of fasting, nights of prayer,
To gird his soul anew.
And sometimes would the wind-borne chime
Of chaunted hymn in the still night-time,
Far floating, reach the awe-struck ear
Of the lone sailing mariner.
Other times on the headland high,
When sunset made earth, sea, and sky
One blended glory, there far seen,
Appeared, men said, his form and mien,
All glistening with celestial sheen;
No light, I ween, from this world's sun,
But a foregleam of heaven begun.
When many a vigil, toil, and fast
Had worn his frame ere noon of age
Was reached, from that dark cave he past
Up to the better heritage.
And when he died in yon green glen
They laid him down beside the river,

And that became to future men
  A place of hallowed rest for ever.
Columba from his isle of Y
  A psalm of blessing chaunted o'er him,
And Aidan, of Dalriad race
The foremost king, this resting-place
  Chose, for the love he bore him.

IV.

Three centuries on, King Kenneth rose,
  And o'er Drum-Albin east away
Passed to war down his Pictish foes
  At Luncarty, by the holms of Tay;
And with him went that fateful stone,
  Whereof the ancient Weirds ordain,
That, where it stands, shall stand a throne,
  On which the Scottish line shall reign.
They passed, and left this western shore,
  Seat of a royal race no more.
But soon were seen the snowy sails
  Of the Fiongall, those Northmen tall,
Azure eyed, with streaming hair,
And pagan hearts that would not spare,
Spread on the roaring northern gales.
From the great main, down the Minch, they sped,
  Raking the islands, creek and cape,
From Butt-of-Lewes to Barra-head,
And all the Inner isles outspread—
  A storm none living might escape.

No help, no pity; before them fell
The wattled hut, the Culdee's cell;
In holy place of Y the priest
Lay slaughtered, and the worship ceased;
The light good men had kindled there
Was trampled out; no voice of prayer,
No chaunt of hymn for centuries
Was heard amid these moaning seas.

Then Norroway Kings, our chiefs o'erthrown,
Held isle and islet for their own,
  And one, more haughty than the rest,
Swore he would claim for island ground
Whate'er he drove his galley round;
  And from the Atlantic up the west
Loch Tarbert bearing, made them haul
His barge across that isthmus small,
  Himself proud-seated at the helm;
Then spreading sail down fair Loch Fyne,
He cried aloud "Kintyre is mine,
  I've bound it to my island-realm."

VI.

At last rose Somerled the brave,
And bursting from the mountain cave
That was his cradle, to his call
Gathered our Celtic people all,
  And falling on the Northmen, drave

Them stricken from the mountains brown
Of Morven to the ocean down;
  There where he laid each strong one low,
By rock, and scaur, and torrent fall,
Still live their names, memorial
  Of that mighty overthrow.
Lord of Kintyre, Prince of Argyll—
'Twas thus he took the kingly style—
And great in power, more great in pride,
To battle Scotland's King defied,
Headstrong, and resolute to maintain
His kinsman's right to rule as Thane,
Or Maormar, Moray's wide domain.
Thereafter up the Firth of Clyde
  With a great host he bore,
And sire and son fell side by side,
  On Renfrew's fateful shore.
They rowed him home, and in the glen
  Of Saddell made his grave,
Behind his own grim castle-keep,
That on its jagg'd rock breasts the sweep
  Of the plashing wave.
There 'neath a blue stone, graven o'er
With plaided warrior and claymore,
Beside the abbey's ivied piles
Long sleeps the first Lord of the Isles.

VII.

Cleft into many branches, spread
  Through all the isles and mainland shore.

The line of lordly Somerled,
Still waxing more and more.
High Ruarie rose, and Lorn—but higher
That other rose, and broader grew,
The House of Islay and Kintyre,
As age by age they drew
Their kinsmen's strength within their own.
To build themselves an island throne.
Kingly their state in Islay green,
When many a vassal, chief and clan,
Thronged from far homes mid ocean wild,
Around their castle, doubly-isled,
Lone 'mid the Loch of Finlagan ;
Or to their mainland towers that frowned
At Saddell o'er Kilbrannan Sound,
Or at strong-walled Dunaverty,
Out looking on the wide west sea.

VIII.

Hither The Bruce, when sore bestead,
From vengeful Lorn, and Southron foes,
By Nigel Campbell guided, fled
And found a brief repose.
Breadalbane gave no shelter. Lorn
Had hurled him back with hate and scorn,
And Lennox mountains, with their Earl,
Though true of heart, availèd not ;
Kintyre alone kept safe from peril,
One sure and sheltered spot,

To welcome him, one fortress freed
From danger, for his utmost need.
There, Angus, Lord of Innisgall,
Him and his men in friendly hall
Received, and feasted full days three,
Within the towered Dunaverty,
By the margin of the wild west sea.
The Campbell and the Macdonald met
  Firm friends and leal that day:
They dreamt not how their sons would wage
Fierce feud through many a future age,
  In many a deadly fray.
Together they rowed to lone Rathrin
  The King long months to lie,
And watch there the weird spider spin
  Her thread of destiny;
That thread which held the ay or no
Of Scotland's endless weal or woe.

IX.

And when the king from the lone isle
  Went forth to backward turn
The tide of warfare, and to cast
That die, the weightiest and the last,
  By the Bannockburn;
Again these met, mid battle broil.
Yoke-fellows in the glorious toil,
  That made Scotland free.

Men tell, how as he ranged his host.
The good king turned to see,
If Angus with his people came,
And hailed him with that kind acclaim,
'My hope is firm in thee;'
That word of trust henceforth became
MacDonald's ensenzie.
Then Bruce struck Lorn's proud chieftain down
With Comyn banded 'gainst his crown,
And to Sir Neil and Angus gave
The rebels' power o'er land and wave
By all this western sea.
These parted then, and not again
MacDonald with the Campbell met,
But ages long aloof they stood,
Each feeding his own separate mood
In sternest contrast set.

..

The House of Islay royally dowered
With a Princess for a bride,
Broader spread and loftier towered
In too o'erweening pride.
And when Earl Ross in grave was laid,
And none to heir his name,
A vow to die great Donald made,
Or else sustain his claim.
Then the western billows, miles on miles,
'Neath barge and bierlin roared,

As the valiant war-men of the Isles
To Donald's standard poured.
Sae brave a host! the like again
The Hielans never saw,
When Donald with ten thousand men
Marched down to the dread Harlaw.
Mailed cavaliers and lowland lords
Rade down our ranks amain,
But our plaided men with their good broadswords
Clave their helm'd heads in twain.
A hail lang simmer day right on
They fought, and did not yield,
And ruddy ran the streams of Don
With the carnage of that field.
And all along the Garioch there
Lay mony a braw knicht slain,
And mony an islesman never mair
Saw the misty isles again.
Ay! sair and lang the Hielans mourned,
And still men mind with awe,
The brave who went, and not returned
From the 'red field of Harlaw.'

XI.

But still renewed that ancient feud
From sire to son went down,
Till the fourth James in strength arose,
And launched against his island foes
The whole might of the crown.

In vain against their doom they fought—
That House divided, self-distraught,
Like a full river-flood, that, cleft
In many streams, hath failed,
Of its high-lineaged Head bereft,
To manifold confusion left,
Not any more availed.
The last lord of the haughty line,
Fain lifelong tumult to resign,
Sought Paisley's still abbaye ;
And there, of all ambition shriven,
Found rest perchance power ne'er had given,
For life's declining day.
That warrior race still lives this hour,
But shorn of its once kinglike power ;
The Lord of the Isles, a name of yore
Dear to the Gael, is known no more.

XII.

And yet though proud those Island lords,
Though endless were their combatings,
Now with vassals, and savage hordes,
Now with Scotland's kings,
Yet ever at core of their rougher heart
Lay some more tender, reverent, part.
Their sea-towers fronted wave and wind
On the headland grim ;
The convent slept in the glen behind,
'Mid tree shadows dim ;

The Castle for their stormy life,
The Convent for its close,
That with battle and bloodshed rife,
This keeping for them, who were done with strife.
Shelter and long repose.
In Saddell glen, a fair abbaye
They built, that prayer night and day
Might rise from Somerled's place of rest,
And Lord and Chieftain, age by age,
Enlarged the sacred heritage
By dower and bequest.
A copsewood here, a fishing there,
Small island or hill-pasture fair,
They gave in part or whole.
Perchance, they thought to soothe the dead.
Perchance, to win, when life was fled,
Peace for their earth-stained soul.
So to these Churchmen made they o'er
A portion of this lee'ar-side shore,
Eilau Davar, the island bold,
And on the mainland, high and low,
Fields and braes, to have and hold,
Of bonny Kilmahoe.
Saint Ciaran's presence seemed to brood,
And hallow all this solitude,
And so with pious care
They built them up on yonder brae,
From the Saint's cave not far away
A little cell for prayer.

A sound of peace that belfry sent,
  Where seldom peace was known ;
As down these shores its calm voice went,
And touched rude hearts and turbulent,
  With its soul-awing tone.

XIII.

The Campbell Clan had other fate
  Than the proud House of Somerled,
Since first Lochow's good knight, Sir Neil,
True to the Bruce through woe and weal,
  The King's own sister wed.
Waiting, not struggling to be great,
  To loyal duty bred,
The Kings they served, as men of state,
  Or hosts to battle led :
One Earl marched forth, with all his clan.
  To Flodden's war-array,
And with our fiery Highland van
Dashed down the steep, the foremost man,
  To death that rueful day ;
Him, and Glen Urquhay's kindred knight,
Their clansmen far from the wasteful fight
Bore home, and side by side they lie
By Saint Mun's ruined chapelry.

XIV.

Wary of heart, and strong of hand,
  Shrewd to gain, and sure to keep,

Gathering vassals, widening land,
They laid foundations deep;
O'er Lorn, Cowal, Knapdale, reign by reign
They broadened out their old domain,
But had not to their full height grown.
Till the Island Kings were overthrown.
Many a year of rage and grief,
The Islesmen strove against that fall,
To reinstate the attainted chief,
True heir of Ross and Innisgall.
Most fiercely they, Clan-Ian-vor,
Sprung from that son to whom his sire,
Lord of the Isles, consigned of yore
The Chiefdom of Kintyre.
Ay! restless, proud, Clan-Ian-vor,
Kept the old bearing of the Isles,
While closer each Mac-Cailein-mor
Drew round the net-work of state-wiles;
As hunters wear a herd of deer
From windy peaks and bare hillsides
Down to a pass where every rock
A deadly ambush hides,
He watched their temper, bode the hour
For his long-brooded plan,
Then, backed with all the kingdom's power,
Let slip his straining clan.
Relentless as unleashed bloodhounds,
They plied with sword and fire,

And hunted from their ancient grounds
Of Islay and Kintyre
The outlawed MacDonalds,—wildly rang
Their conflict—down these mountain shores
The fiery cross flew,—then the clang
Of slogans and claymores.
Nor ceased the slaughtering, till Argyll
His long-sought purpose surely gained—
This mainland, and that Kingly Isle,
Where erst Clandonald reigned.

XV.

But when King Charles prelatic yoke
Would thrust on Scotland—blindly wrong—
Mac-Cailein-mor and his people broke
With the Stuarts they had served so long.
A chief was he, most wise to wield
State counsels 'mid a nation's throes,
But could not stand in battle-field
Before the great Montrose.
Ye've heard, I ween, of that last meeting,
How from the Graham's too gallant greeting
Recoiled the stricken Campbell host,
All headlong down Lochaber coast.
There steadfast 'mid that rout and wreck,
Your own forefather nobly died,
The trusty knight of Auchinbreck,
Under Ben Nevis' side.

'Twas then from Inverlochy's fray
  The remnant of Clan-Ian-vor,
Athirst for vengeance, burst away
  To the lands they held of yore.
They swept Argyll, and slew, and slew,
  Harrying homes and bearing spoil,
And forward, unresisted, flew
  Down to the utmost Moil.
Every soul of Campbell name
They gave to sword, their roofs to flame,
There was no hearth unsoaked in blood,
This land was one waste solitude.

XVI.

Argyll and Lesley were not slack·
Sternly to pay that outrage back;
When leaguered by that western sea,
In the strong-walled Dunaverty,
Those clansmen famishing implored
Mercy, and found the merciless sword.
Even where they fell, their bleached bones lie
Under the castle, strewn in caves,
Or on the sea-sand, washed by waves.
  Bare to the heaven's broad eye.
The night when that wild work was done,
Of all the clan survived but one,
A child, his nurse faithful and brave
  Bore naked through the frenzied host

And refuged in a sea-cliff cave
  High on the sheer Mull-coast—
Child that in after years became
Rebuilder of the family name.

XVII.

O Leddies! those were fearsome times.
The purest were not clean from crimes;
Yet whate'er dark or doubtful may
Have gathered round their middle way,
At last when sire and son were driven
  For faith and conscience' sake to face
Stern death, they welcomed his embrace
  With calm that breathed of heaven.
Yea, never chief amid his peers,
The war-pipe thundering in his ears,
  More dauntless faced the battle shock.
Than those Argylls, by pure faith made
Serene and strong, their heads down laid
  Upon the Maiden block.

XVIII.

And when time brought the turn of tide.
  Each to his own tradition true,
MacDonald clasped the old and died.
  Argyll went forward with the new.
Then many changed from friends to foes;
  But when their backs were at the wall,

Whom could the Stuarts trust like those,
  Of whom their fathers wrought the fall?
Ay, ever as their cause declined,
  And other friends waxed faint and few,
The more for them our clan combined,
  The stauncher round their standard drew.
They died, the flower of all the Highlands,
  How many a manly heart and pure!
At Inverlochy, Killiekrankie,
  At Sherra, and Culloden, muir;
Ah me! what blood was shed in vain,
The Stuarts ne'er came back again.

XIX.

These stormy ages now are rolled,
  Like tempest clouds from shore and hill;
But, even as mists of evening gold,
  Their memories linger still.
Nor memories only—we are sons
And daughters of those valiant ones,
The brave men who, on either side
Of the great old battles, fought and died.
That Auchinbreck, the leader brave,
  Who fell on Inverlochy plain,
That child, who cradled in sea-cave,
  Raised his fall'n house again;
O Leddies! both these ancient strains
Of blood were in your father's veins.

For ere the wars were overblown,
  Transplanted to this hill-side lea,
From Auchinbreck a shoot had grown,
With the Chief's shelter round it thrown,
  To be a stalwart tree.
And when with peace old foes grew kind,
  A fair young flower, from Sanda brought,
About that roof-tree intertwined,
  With many a blessing fraught.
O happy wind! O healing tide!
  O day of joy to high and low!
That wafted o'er the winsome bride
  From Sanda's isle to Kilmahoe.
When wed the fair Macdonald maid
  And the Christian pastor, wise and mild,
In them the ancient strife was stayed,
  The long feud reconciled.
And in their child, your honoured sire,
  From either race old virtues bloomed
To flower of manhood, fairer, higher,
  By light from heaven illumed.
It seemed, as though on this lone shore,
  Clan feuds and violence all foregone,
Saint Ciaran's faith, relit once more,
  In his pure spirit shone.
And naught I doubt, though long delayed,
  On earth from age to age there dawns,
That for which saints have toiled and prayed,
  In lives of holy ones.

IX.

THE GARDEN.

THE bielded garden close behind
Lies nestling, girt with hoary trees,
And backed by hills that keep all wind
Aloof, save the soft southern breeze;
There consecrate to quiet and ease,
Year by year, doth that garden lie,
Far removed from all the press
And throng of life, an open eye
Of beauty 'mid the wilderness.
There many a flower unknown elsewhere,
And many a delicate plant and rare,
Loves to breathe the moist mild air;
There the timorous myrtle nothing fears
The edge of winter's half-sheathed shears,
But hearing early the call of spring
Wakens to starry blossoming;
There the fuchsia thinking scorn to be
A low shrub, towers a bowery tree,
'Neath which the children, at their play
Of hide-and-seek, large covert gain,
And even grown men on a showery day
Find shelter from the chiming rain;

The al[illegible]d, mindful of her time,
Drink[illegible]alth and joy from the warm sea air,
And d[illegible], as in southern clime,
In spr[illegible] doth blossom, in autumn bear.

Thi[illegible]orning to the warm May sun
The [illegible] garden, like an incense cup,
Innu[illegible]erous odours, blent in one
Rich [illegible]grant steam, is breathing up,
An[illegible] giving them to the young winds o'er,
To waft aloof
O'er the old home roof,
A [illegible]nge of odour to sea and shore.

Othe[illegible]hings than odours come,
Othe[illegible]ounds than the live hum
Of b[illegible], this noon from the garden walk;
Murr[illegible]rous sounds of happy talk
And [illegible]ughter-peals thro' the light leaves throng.
or [illegible]assed away are the dripping, long
Dar[illegible]vinter heavens, and warm and clear
Blue[illegible]ies shine out, and the swallows are here:
And [illegible]ith them sisters clustering round
Him [illegible]he long-lost, lately found
Brot[illegible]r, for whom their souls had yearned
Too [illegible]eply, to their love returned.
The[illegible] are the voices now we hear
Fro[illegible] the garden come i' the sweet o' the year
On [illegible] her arm hangs one entwined,
All [illegible]ng upon his looks and words,

Moira before, and Marion behind
Their voices, like young swallow rds.
When at morn from the thatched aves
Come their sweet-throated falls a heaves:
So this noon they weave with sou l
Of happy talk their old home round.

From the garden forth they pass
Out among the orchard grass,
Beneath the pear and apple trees
White with blossom,—where the bees
With new-wakened vernal hum
From the mountains go and come
And every breath from off the boughs
Blows drifts of rosy-tinted snows—
On to the central old pear tree
Of all Kintyre the patriarch; he,
Hoary and hollowed by the touch
Of centuries, had o'er-lived so much,
Of trees and men seen disappear
Whole generations—undismayed—
Himself still brave to welcome here
Another 'neath his giant shade:
There all their childhood they had made
A glad resort for out-door play,
And hour on hour had whiled away;
Now instinct-led their footsteps strayed
Thither, as to a sacred hearth,
The centre of their native earth.

The almond, mindful of her time,
Drinks health and joy from the warm sea air.
And duly, as in southern clime,
In spring doth blossom, in autumn bear.

This morning to the warm May sun
The old garden, like an incense cup,
Innumerous odours, blent in one
Rich fragrant steam, is breathing up,
And giving them to the young winds o'er,
To waft aloof
O'er the old home roof,
A fringe of odour to sea and shore.

Other things than odours come,
Other sounds than the live hum
Of bees, this noon from the garden walk;
Murmurous sounds of happy talk
And laughter-peals thro' the light leaves throng.
For cleansed away are the dripping, long
Dark, winter heavens, and warm and clear
Blue skies shine out, and the swallows are here:
And with them sisters clustering round
Him, the long-lost, lately found
Brother, for whom their souls had yearned
Too deeply, to their love returned.
Theirs are the voices now we hear
From the garden come i' the sweet o' the year
On either arm hangs one entwined,
All hang upon his looks and words,

Moira before, and Marion behind,
Their voices, like young swallow birds,
When at morn from the thatchèd eaves
Come their sweet-throated falls and heaves:
So this noon they weave with sound
Of happy talk their old home round.

From the garden forth they pass
Out among the orchard grass,
Beneath the pear and apple trees
White with blossom,—where the bees
With new-wakened vernal hum
From the mountains go and come,
And every breath from off the boughs
Blows drifts of rosy-tinted snows—
On to the central old pear tree
Of all Kintyre the patriarch; he,
Hoary and hollowed by the touch
Of centuries, had o'er-lived so much,
Of trees and men seen disappear
Whole generations—undismayed—
Himself still brave to welcome here
Another 'neath his giant shade:
There all their childhood they had made
A glad resort for out-door play,
And hour on hour had whiled away;
Now instinct-led their footsteps strayed
Thither, as to a sacred hearth,
The centre of their native earth.

School-time ended, weary time,
In south England, far from home,
Ere a longer exile come
To another farther clime,
Rest here awhile, thou ruddy boy!
Curlèd darling of thy race,
Home-hearts feel a vernal joy
Forth-flowing from thy sunny face;
In huts of poor men, far and near,
By shore or corry, blithelier burn
The ingles, old cheeks gather cheer,
At the glad news of thy return.

O seldom seen, but passing sweet
Hour, when the broken family meet,
And gaze, within the ancestral door,
On a long-lost face returned once more.
The river of home-love is full,
And fain within this trancèd pool
Would linger on, content to brood
For ever o'er its blissful mood,
Not knowing what in store may be,
Of brawl or thwarting rock, below,
Or headlong fall, when it shall go
Its voyage to the infinite sea;
But fearing, life may bring no bliss
So solid, and so pure, as this.

Ah days! that come but once a life,

Yet with all blessèd memories rife,
Ye quickly pass, yet never die,
But deep within our being lie
Like some fair garden ground, to breathe
Far-wafted fragrance, and bequeath
A heritage down all our years
Of calmer smiles and mellower tears.

And meaning more than fond regret
Comes with these thoughts of meetings past
That will not be again—they cast
Far on beyond earth's narrow scope
A longing look, a hint, a hope,
To some good end undreamed of yet,
Some day far on, when all the sore
Farewells of earth shall be known no more,
And all long human yearning stilled,
At the fountain-head of love fulfilled.

But, sisters, take what little space
The unclouded light from that glad face
Falls on you, take it all for joy;
Since festal hours of childhood time
Will not be here for ever,—climb
These breezy hills with your brother boy,
And, foreheads bare, from height to height
Range on in all-day-long delight,
With gladness strewing the mountain winds,
Till the shy red roes and the listening hinds,

Down in the corries and hazelly glens,
At your laughter start from their ferny dens,
Take all for joy, nor scare away
With boding thought the too brief to-day.
Ask not—Oh! well ye may not see,
The issue of the years to be,
Whether he large wealth shall earn,
And a hoary man to these hills return,
Or lay him down in an unknown grave,
O'er which Indian palm-trees wave.

X.

THE SACRAMENTAL SABBATH.

'Mid the folding mountains,
Old Kilcieran's lone kirkyard
Round its ruin'd chapel gathers,
Age by age, the grey hill-fathers
Underneath the heathery sward.

Centuries gone the saint from Erin
Hither came on Christ's behest,
Taught and toiled, and when was ended
Life's long labour, here found rest;
And all ages since have followed
To the ground his grave hath blessed.

Up the long glen narrowing
Inland from the eastern deep,
In the kirkyard o'er the river,
Where dead generations sleep,
Living men on summer Sabbaths
Worship long have loved to keep.

There o'er graves lean lichened crosses,
Placed long since by hands unknown,

Sleeps the ancient warrior under
The blue claymore-sculptured stone,
And the holy well still trickles
From rock basin, grass-o'ergrown.

Lulled the sea this Sabbath morning,
Calm the golden-misted glens,
And the white clouds upward passing
Leave unveiled the azure Bens,
Altars pure to lift to heaven
Human hearts' unheard amens.

And the folk are flowing
Both from near and far, enticed
By old wont and reverent feeling
Here to keep the hallowed tryst,
This calm sacramental Sabbath,
Far among the hills, with Christ.

Dwellers on this side the country
Take the shore-road, near their doors,
Poor blue-coated fishers, plaided
Crofters from the glens and moors,
Fathers, mothers, sons, and daughters.
Hither trooping, threes and fours.

Plaids were there that only Sabbath
Saw, and wives' best tartan hoods,
Grannies' white coifs, and bareheaded

Maidens with their silken snoods;
Many-hued, home-woven tartans,
Brightening these grave solitudes.

You might see on old white horses
Agèd farmers slowly ride,
With their wives behind them seated,
And the collie by their side;
While the young folk follow after,
Son and daughter, groom and bride

There a boat or two is coming
From lone isle or headland o'er,
Many more, each following other,
Slowly pull along the shore,
Fore and aft to gunwale freighted
With the old, the weak, the poor,

The bowed down, the lame, the palsied,
Those with panting breath opprest,
Widows poor, in mutch and tartan
Cloak, for one day lent them, drest,
And the young and ruddy mother,
With the bairnie at her breast.

And the western shores Atlantic,
All the rough side of Kintyre,
Send small bands since morn, far-travelled
O'er hill, river, moss, and mire,

Down the mountain shoulders moving
Toward this haven of their desire.

Sends each glen and hidden corry,
As they pass, its little train,
To increase the throng that thickens
Kirkward, like the growing gain
From hill-burns, which some vale-river
Broadening beareth to the main.

While the kirkyard throng and thronger
Groweth, some their kindred greet;
Others in lone nooks and corners
To some grass-grown grave retreat,
There heed not the living, busy
With the dead beneath their feet.

Here on green mound sits a widow,
Rocking crooningly to and fro,
Over him with whom so gladly
To God's house she used to go;
There the tears of wife and husband
Blend o'er a small grave below.

There you might o'erhear some old man
Palsied speaking to his son,
'See thou underneath this headstone
Make my bed, when all is done,
There long since I laid my father,
There his forebears lie, each one.'

They too, all the kindly household
From morn-gladdened Kilmahoe,
Steek their door, and maid and mistress,
Toward the Sabbath gathering go,
Lady lone, and four fair daughters,
By the lulled sea murmuring low.

Upward from the shingly sea-beach,
By the long glen's grassy road,
First the white-haired lady mother,
Then the elder sisters, trode,
Last came Moira fair, and Marion,
All their spirits overawed.

Meek and very lowly
Souls, bowed down with reverent fear,
This their first communion day!
To the awful presence holy
Dread it is to draw so near,
Pain it were to turn away.

So, of old, the Hebrew maiden,
'Mid the Galilean mountains
Leaving all her childhood time,
With her kinsfolk, incense-laden,
By Kedron's brook, Siloah's fountain,
Zion hill awe-struck would climb.

As they pass within the kirk-yard,
Some old e es long used to stoo

Rose and brightened on these maidens,
Youngest of the family group,
Marion's flaxen ringlets, Moira's
Large soft eyes with downward droop.

Loved ones of the country people,
They had dandled them on their knees,
Watched them with their bairnies ranging
The shore coves and mountain leas;
Year by year beheld their beauty
Like a summer dawn increase:
Now on this their first communion
Those old eyes look blessing and peace.

Sweet the chime from ruined belfry
Stealeth; at its peaceful call
Round the knoll whereon the preacher
Takes his stand, they gather all:
In whole families seated, o'er them
Hallowed stillness seems to fall.

There they sit, the men bareheaded
By their wives; in reverence meek
Many an eye to heaven is lifted,
Many lips, not heard to speak,
Mutely moving, on their worship
From on high a blessing seek.

Some on grey-mossed headstones seated,

S

Grave-browed men and tartaned matrons
Swell the mighty Celtic psalm,
On from glen to peak repeated,
Far into the mountain calm.

Then the aged pastor rose,
White with many a winter's snows
Fallen o'er his ample brows;
And his voice of pleading prayer,
Cleaving slow the still blue air,
All his people's need laid bare.

Laden with o'erflowing feeling
Then streamed on his fervid chaunt,
In the old Highland tongue appealing
To each soul's most hidden want
With the life and deep soul-healing,
He who died now lives to grant.

Slow the people round the table
Outspread, white as mountain sleet,
Gather, the blue heaven above them,
And their dead beneath their feet,
There in perfect reconcilement
Death and life immortal meet.

Noiseless round that fair white table
'Mid their fathers' tombstones spread,
Hoary-headed elders moving,

While devoutly still the people
Low in prayer bow the head.

Tender hearts, their first communion,
Many a one was in that crowd;
With them in mute adoration,
Breathless Moira and Marion bowed,
While far up on yon blue summit
Paused the silver cloud.

And no sound was heard—save only
Distance-lulled the Atlantic roar,
Over the calm mountains coming
From far Machrahanish shore,
Like an audible eternity
Brooding the hushed people o'er.

Soon they go—but ere another
Day of hallowed bread and wine,
Some now here shall have ascended
To communion more divine,
Some have changed their old hill-dwellings,
Some have swept the tropic line.

Several of the above incidents are taken from a beautiful Gaelic paper, descriptive of a like scene, written for his 'Teachdair Gaidhealach,' by the late Dr. Macleod of St. Columba's.

XI.

THE PARTING.

I.

Go, Sisters, sweet Sisters, and gather
  For Moira, the bonny May,
Wild flowers to busk her sunny-brown hair,
  This her bridal day.
That small white star-flower gather,
  Lover of lonely fells,
The earliest flush of the summer heather,
  The choice of the young blue-bells.

II.

Why bid us bright garlands weave?
  Looks of gladness feign?
Can they win for our souls one hour's reprieve
  From the pang of the parting pain?

III.

Yet though your hearts be breaking,
  Bright your faces keep,
To-day for laughter and loud mirth-making,
  To-morrow long time to weep.

Hark! how the woodland birds
Her bridal morning hail!
Then why those timorous whispered words?
Ah! why those cheeks so pale?

II.

Well may song-birds be waking
This new morn to greet,
Of them no sister is long leave taking,
Or they would not sing so sweet.
A boat lies on yonder beach,
There a ship flaps seaward sail,—
Therefore this low and timorous speech,
Therefore these cheeks so pale.

[illegible].

Bring her forth in her bridal attire,
Yourselves in white raiment clad,
She the bonniest May of all Kintyre,
He a gallant lowland lad.
Ere his eighteenth year was o'er,
Far in the eastern world,
The British colours alone he bore
In the battle van unfurled.
If the bloom of his cheek be marred
By the bronze of the Indian sun,
Yet his brows are wreathed and his breast is starred
For the deeds he there hath done.

He faced the wild war hooves' thunder
'Gainst the squares on Laswarry plain,
He breasted the breach of Bhurtpòre right under
The shot falling thick as rain.

II.

Ah! nothing I doubt that he,
Who loves her, is gentle as brave,
But well I feel, her going must be
Our sweet childhood's grave.

I.

Nay! only she goeth where
Her brother is gone before;
Would you grudge them the joy of their meeting there,
On that Indian shore?

II.

Exile may exile greet
In that far land, and be fain;
But when shall the sundered family meet
In their old home again?

I.

Yet now aside ye must stand,
Who have loaded her with your love,
And yield her o'er to the unseen hand,
Reached down on her from above.

II.

Thou joy of all our race!
   Springtime of all our year!
What is life, if we see not thy fair young face,
   No more thy bright laughter hear?
O soul of all our delights!
   O sunshine of all our days!
How bear without thee the long winter nights?
   How walk the o'erdarkened ways?

I.

The day, it hath come, hath come,
   Ye maun part, for so He wills,
Through bleeding hearts and a broken home
   Who the one end fulfils.
Lead her down, lead her down to the beach,
   Kiss her cheek ere she leave the strand,
She is passing far out of your loving reach,
   Not from the All-guiding Hand.

XII.

MARION TO MOIRA.

MOIRA, sweet sister mine,
  Over the sea
Thou hast ta'en the glad sunshine,
  Left darkness to me.
Spring now is bleak and dull,
Summer not beautiful,
Hueless the flowers we pull,—
  Severed from thee.

We drudge on at duty,
  Hearts cold as stone,
Earth has no beauty,
  Song-birds no tone;
Dimmed is the ocean gleam,
Mournful the mountains seem,
Dolefully falls the stream,
  Since thou art gone.

What hath earth now to give?—
  O sweetest dove!
Never I thought to live,
  Lorn of thy love;

Thou who couldst cheer me,
Hearten, uprear me,
Light ever near me,
  Round, and above!

Long days and nights of care
  Drearly we dree,
Heavy is life to bear,
  Severed from thee.
Loved and long-parted!
True and home-hearted!
When wilt thou, when wilt thou
  Come back to me?

XIII.

MOIRA TO MARION.

Oh! strangely sounds in this far land
  The voice of thy complaining,
To me who oft at evening stand,
  With dimmed eyes westward straining;

And dream, the sun that yonder dies
  Awakes on far-off islands,
And lifts the lids from dear-loved eyes
  Within my own blue Highlands;

Far up on lonely corrie smites
  Grey scarfs of mist to golden,
And down below slants gladsome lights
  Through rooms long unbeholden.

O, then, what yearnings o'er me come!
  Would we too now were leaving
These fiery skies for that cool home,
  Which seems an earthly heaven!

Then comes the thought, where'er He wills,
  There is the best abiding;
Parched sands are better than green hills,
  If His good hand be guiding.

Deem not these words are empty sound,
  Mere common hearsay only;
That they are true I 've tried and found,
  In life's dark hours and lonely,

When in the tent alone I bode,
  And heard the war-gear rattle,
As down the desert far he rode,
  My true love, rode to battle.

In that and many a danger dim,
  'Twas well to wait in meekness,
And roll my whole care o'er on Him,
  Who bringeth strength from weakness.

Then, Sister! though thy days may drag
  Wearily in their going,
Let not thy gentle spirit flag
  In duty, this well knowing,

O'er our dark moods His sunshine broods;
  And though long last the sadness,
In patience wait, and soon or late
  Will break heaven's light and gladness.

Yet may we wander up the glen,
  Yet to the loud linn listen,
Gaze from the old peaks together, when
  The seas in sunset glisten.

But not to hope so frail and fond
  Shall we our hearts deliver,
We, travellers to a home beyond,
  Where who meet, meet for ever.

XIV.

RETURN.

From the top of the mountains
  Lift ye up the voice!
Kilmahoe and the dwellers
  Therein rejoice!

Look forth from the headland
  Of high Auchnahaun;
Beneath, ocean floor kindles
  Bright to the dawn.

Lo! the jagg'd peaks of Arran
  The sun's forehead tips,
And touches with brightness
  The white-wingèd ships,

And far out to sea,
  Like a bright fleck of foam,
Strikes to glory yon sail
  That wafts Moira home.

O blest day of autumn!
  From gates of the east,
The fairest, benignest,
  That e'er was released,

Our hills have long waited—
  Come, strike and illume
Their bosoms of heather,
  Now flushing in bloom;

Rise, shine, gladness bringing
  To land and to sea,
And Moira, the longed for,
  The lovely, to me.

Ye soft southland winds!
  Give the bark fuller way;
Still faster, ye boatmen!
  Back fling the oar-spray;

Till grates in the shingle
  The prow of the barge,
Where yearning hearts wait
  By the sounding sea marge.

Since, a bride newly wed,
  She passed forth from that shore,
Wild with weeping farewells,
  Seven summers are o'er.

To-day on that sea-beach
  The hearts that long yearned
Overflow tears of joy
  For their darling returned.

Ah! simple and long
  Are the faiths that they keep,
The roots of their love
  Strike more clingingly deep,

Whose childhood hath grown
  By calm mountains enfurled,
Not tossed on turmoil
  Of a feverish world.

She who left with the tender
  Spring-bloom on her face,
Steps ashore in full summer
  Of matronly grace,

Through war, plague, and tempest
  Safe-shielded from harm;
A bairn at her knee,
  And a babe in her arm;

With her soldier brought back
  From the lands of the sun,
His manly cheek paled,
  But his battles all done.

Lead them up, lead them onward,
  Across the green field,
And by the wood path
  Through the hazel shaw bield.

Lead them up, lead them on,
  Open wide the home door,
'Neath its lintel ne'er passed
  So glad comers before.

Ah! well may ye gaze
  On that face; it hath passed
Through strange peoples, wild scenes,
  Since ye looked on it last:

Through old cities of Ind,
  Where the swart natives crowd,
With willing salaams
  Round their conquerors bowed,

She hath passed; to hearts worn
  With that fierce tropic clime,
Like a breeze freshly blowing
  From mountains of thyme:

'Mid the gay and the careless
  In court, camp, and ball,
Untrammelled by any,
  Belovèd of all:

Been doomed in heart sickness,
  All helpless, to hear
The battle her lord led on
  Hurtling anear :—

Hath ridden, for days and nights,
  Vast deserts dim,
And stemmed on her steed
  Brimming rivers with him :

Hath seen off Mozambique
  The foe full in chase,
Bear down on their frail bark
  To deadly embrace ;

And from Gallic two-deckers
  The broadsides inpoured,
Till rent yard and reeling mast
  Went by the board :

Felt far in mid-ocean
  The shuddering shock,
As the vessel went grinding
  Stem on to the rock ;

Then calm and undaunted
  In stern face of death,
Shed calmness around
  By the meek might of faith.

But after the tempest's o'er,
  Cometh the calm;
After long day labour
  Sleep's blessed balm;

After world-wandering
  Home-welcome pure;
After life's fitful stir
  Rest to endure.

All that day in the garden
  And high woodland walk,
All that eve in the old rooms
  Flowed sweet warbling talk;

Like a burn hidden down
  In a dell of green leaves,
Or low gurgle of swallows
  That nest in the eaves:

While the old lady looked,
  From the chimney-side chair,
With large eyes undimmed
  'Neath her white braided hair,

Mute thankful amaze
  On her far-wandered dove,
Flown back o'er the stormy seas
  Home to her love;

With two little lives,
  For her eyes to repose
On their beauty brief while,
  Ere for ever they close.

XV.

SPRING AND AUTUMN.

If thou hast ranged the woodlands in the first
Fair fledging of the leaves, when Spring is new,
Hast thou not paused in wonder, how they burst
Various in shape and hue?

There is one glory of the shimmering birk,
One of the beech-tree's bright transparent sheen,
One of the linden's golden fairy-work,
One of the plane's pure green.

Even in the self-same kind, each tree endued
Shines with its several colour,—oaks outspread,
Some rich bronzed leafage, some green golden-hued,
And some deep purple-red.

Quickly these bright hues pass; but come again,
When summer suns have made their work complete,
And, from some high craig of wide-stretching ken,
Lay Trossach pass, or Killiecrankie glen,
Unrolled beneath thy feet;

What time the frosty-bright October lays
  Transfiguring hand on wild wood bank and brae,
Kindling the copses to a rich calm blaze,
  A glory of decay:

All hues, made brighter in the clear still air,
  Light amber, pale green, golden, russet-brown,
With scarlet dashed and purple, waiting there
  Till the storm-wind come down.

Like to the trees are we: our youth and age
  Hint plainly what will be, and what hath been;
But the long summer of life's middle stage
  Fulfils its growth unseen.

So pass we o'er the time that each descends
  From the home nook into the wide world-school,
That school which tries us singly, while it blends
  All under one stern rule;

Yea, tries and tests our being through and through;
  And yet so uniform the outward guise,
That what we are may be discerned by few,
  And these, familiar eyes;

Till the ripe autumn of the soul hath brought
  Its mellow colouring,—then the very grain
And hue, by life's long purpose inly wrought,
  Comes out distinct and plain,

What we have made it. Who in selfish cares
And worldly ways have all their noon outworn,
I'm loath to think what evening must be theirs,
How cold and heart-forlorn!

But they, the kindly, pure, and true, who have had
Their hidden root in Him who is The Truth,
They even to their hoar hairs shall be glad,
As with the dews of youth.

XVI.

INGATHERING.

From Kilmahoc there is a brightness gone,
The days are rainier, drearier than before,
More mournfully the grey sea murmurs on
        Against the caverned shore.

And they are gone, who loved that home so well,
Some to far lands, more to the old kirkyard,
And strangers now, who 'neath their roof-tree dwell,
        Them know not, nor regard.

But there 's a Lowland home, where many a year
The bonny Moira's footsteps on the stair,
Among her bairns, and household folk asteer,
        Made music late and air;

An old white lofty-gabled Lowland home:
Up to the sunshine, and the breezes all,
For ages o'er the ancestral trees have clomb
        Its stalwart chimneys tall.

Far seen, for open on the south it gleams
To clear noons, like a white unfurlèd flag;
In rainy weather, dimmed with stains and seams,
Like a grey lichened crag.

Far seen, wide gazing, the old mansion grey,
Adown the long lime avenue, from its doors,
Looks, here to rich tilled lands, yonder, away
To meditative moors.

Hard by, hedge-sheltered garden, hiding woods,
And morning fields, for childhood's summer play,
Nor less responsive to more sober moods,
And life's autumnal day.

In that old home lived Moira, tender wife
And mother, by meek faith and ceaseless prayer,
For them she loved through all the strain of life
Made strong to do and bear.

And when forenoons were over, home tasks done,
Still young in love of nature she would fare
Forth to the fields, to see the setting sun,—
Drink in sweet evening air;

Yet turning oft aside to cottage nook,
Some frail or drooping one to help or cheer;
That was the gentlest voice, the kindest look,
That came there all the year.

It

To her none worthier seemed for being great,
Nor any less because their place was low;
True to that simple, pure heart-estimate,
Which doth not earth's rank know.

Yea! weak things of the world to her were dear,
And the world's gain was emptiness and loss,
As to a heart attuned to overhear
Low music from the cross.

And yet to all so loving: when, keen-eyed
To others' faults, some hastened to condemn,
Her kind heart still some hidden good descried,
And gently pled for them.

To homely Sabbath worships, week by week,
Her way she took, 'neath bright or darkened skies,
And listening there with patient ear, and meek,
She grew more humbly wise.

For her there had not needed dark heart-throes
Of agony; simplest Bible words sufficed,
And griefs that come to all, to bring her close,
And closer still to Christ.

The earthly vessel was by nature fine,
And, early, light of God found entrance there,
And all life's wear not dimmed, but made it shine
More clear and heavenly fair;

Till even worldly hearts, least like to her,
Albeit the while they little seemed to heed,
When they no more beheld her, would aver
She Christian was indeed;

And country people whensoe'er they spoke
Her name, by farmer's hearth or cottar's shed,
Would call her 'the gude Leddy,' and invoke
A blessing on her head.

At length, as on a garden one night's frost
Comes down, and blights the flowers in the fall,
A sudden ailment fell on her; almost
She heard the angel's call.

But God to her life's book one little page
In mercy added, that her own might see,
Who early seek him, in declining age
How beautiful they be;

That all her family, with fond patient heed,
Each gathering round, might know and inly feel,
To whate'er issues other paths may lead,
This way lies endless weal.

As one, who long laboriously going
Beneath a sultry sun up sheer hill slope,
Finds the path easier, fresher breezes blowing,
Just ere he reach the cope:

Even so to her, after long faithful care,
And much meek sorrow, even here was given
A little breathing as of Sabbath air,
Upon the verge of heaven.

She, too, the earliest, as the latest friend,
Her sister playmate on the Highland braes,
Came to the home of Moira, there to tend
The evening of her days.

For she had lived for others, one by one
Had watched them fade, the dear ones of her house,
And propped their failing feet, then wept alone
Above their darkened brows.

She came to see the rose blush, once so sweet,
Pale on the cheek, the dreamlight all gone dim
In those rich eyes, the life-blood feeblier beat
Through every pulse and limb ;

Albeit their orbs, the flushing hues all gone,
Had won a far-off spiritual range,
A pensive depth of peace, as resting on
Things beyond time and change,

Yet full of human tenderness, that drew
All hearts to her ; the old smile lingering yet,
Seemed to wish good, here and hereafter too,
To every soul she met.

And still the high white brow serenely bent
Wore calm that crowns long duty meekly done
O'er faded lineaments with a light not lent
By any earthly sun.

A year and more, they two beneath that roof
Mingled the memories bright from Kilmahoe
With calm thoughts fetched from that still world aloof,
Whereto they soon must go.

At times when all were gathered round the blaze,
In nights of later autumn, she forsook
Her seat beside them, long to stand and gaze,
From the deep window nook,

On the hairst moon, that from alcove of blue
Silvered the garden, every bower and bield,
Hedges of glistening holly and dark yew;
And up the household field

Slanted the shadows of twin silver firs
To white sheep couching on the moon-bathed sward,
Till thought was lost in years that once were hers,—
A far and fond regard.

And oft when nor' winds round the gables blew,
In their low talk beside the gloamin' fire,
Fair faces long since faded smiled anew,
And old days of Kintyre.

In summer from the odorous garden walks,
Or from cool seats o'ershadowed by ash-trees,
Would come the murmur of their quiet talks,
Blended with hum of bees.

Those old springs down the Leear'side, primrose nooks,
And coves that rang with pleasant voices then,
And elder faces meeting them, with looks
Of love long gone from men,

All the fresh fragrance of that early time,
Lived once more on their memory and their tongue,
All their long wanders o'er the hills of thyme,
When limb and heart were young.

Many a scene conn'd o'er, hour brought to mind,
And dear name named for the last time on earth,
Then to the grave of their mute thoughts consigned,
Till the new heavens have birth.

And when the end was come, and only truth
Might go with her down the death-shadowed vale,
He whom she leaned on from her dawn of youth
That dread hour did not fail.

Then in that home was sorrow, not despair:
Like goes to like, and she had gone within,
One dweller more among the many there,
Her spiritual kin;

Blending that season of first yellowing leaves,
And ripe ingathering the bright land abroad,
With thought, how safe are stored His holy sheaves
In the garner-house of God.

But five more years had Marion, not to rest
By kindred graves, within the land she loved,
But yet once more, on duty and love's behest,
To southern shores removed.

Those whom her childhood leant on, one by one,
On their far voyage she had sent before,
And now, for her own summons, all alone,
Stood waiting on the shore.

But none the less for that, only the more,
Around her life, at every turn, she wove,
By kindness flowing from a tried heart-store,
Daily, new links of love.

Till when the fifth ripe autumn had come round,
Beside another than her childhood's sea,
'Mid English graves a peaceful place she found
'Neath the churchyard elm-tree.

So, sundered wide, yet one in heart, they take
Their quiet rest, till dawn that blessed hour,
When life's long-gathering result shall break
Into immortal flower.

FROM THE HIGHLANDS.

THE MOOR OF RANNOCH.

O'ER the dreary moor of Rannoch
   Calm these hours of Sabbath shine;
But no kirk-bell here divideth
   Week-day toil from rest divine.

Ages pass, but save the tempest,
   Nothing here makes toil or haste;
Busy weeks nor restful Sabbath
   Visit this abandoned waste.

Long ere prow of earliest savage
   Grated on blank Albyn's shore,
Lay these drifts of granite boulders,
   Weather-bleached and lichened o'er.

Beuchaille Etive's furrowed visage.
   To Schihallion looked sublime,
O'er a wide and wasted desert,
   Old and unreclaimed as time.

Yea! a desert wide and wasted,
  Washed by rain-floods to the bones;
League on league of heather blasted,
  Storm-gashed moss, grey boulder-stones;

And along these dreary levels,
  As by some stern destiny placed,
Yon sad lochs of black moss water
  Grimly gleaming on the waste;

East and west, and northward sweeping,
  Limitless the mountain plain,
Like a vast low heaving ocean,
  Girdled by its mountain chain:

Plain, o'er which the kingliest eagle,
  Ever screamed by dark Lochowe,
Fain would droop a laggard pinion,
  Ere he touched Ben-Aulder's brow:

Mountain-girdled,—there Bendoran
  To Schihallion calls aloud,
Beckons he to lone Ben-Aulder,
  He to Nevis crowned with cloud.

Cradled here old Highland rivers,
  Etive, Cona, regal Tay,
Like the shout of clans to battle,
  Down the gorges break away.

And the Atlantic sends his pipers
Up yon thunder-throated glen,
O'er the moor at midnight sounding
Pibrochs never heard by men

Clouds, and mists, and rains before them
Crowding to the wild wind tune,
Here to wage their all-night battle,
Unbeheld by star and moon.

Loud the while down all his hollows,
Flashing with a hundred streams,
Corrie-bah from out the darkness
To the desert roars and gleams.

Sterner still, more drearly driven,
There o' nights the north wind raves,
His long homeless lamentation,
As from Arctic seamen's graves.

Till his mighty snow-sieve shaken
Down hath blinded all the lift,
Hid the mountains, plunged the moorland
Fathom-deep in mounded drift.

Such a time, while yells of slaughter
Burst at midnight on Glencoe,
Hither flying babes and mothers
Perished 'mid the waste of snow.

Countless storms have scrawled unheeded
Characters o'er these houseless moors;
But that night engraven forever
In all human hearts endures.

Yet the heaven denies not healing
To the darkest human things,
And to-day some kindlier feeling
Sunshine o'er the desert flings.

Though the long deer-grass is moveless,
And the corrie-burns are dry;
Music comes in gleams and shadows
Woven beneath the dreaming eye.

Desert not deserted wholly!
Where such calms as these can come,—
Never tempest more majestic
Than this boundless silence dumb.

THE LAD OF LOCH SUNART.

THE boat grates down the shingly shore,
Lay out the oars, make fast the tiller,
Our Cameron crew are stout and true,
Their chief Hugh Cameron, the miller;
Loch Sunart's waves laugh, blue and bright,
The hills look down with still delight,
But the brightest there, most full of joy,
That sunny-hearted Cameron boy.

Ben Nevis from his mighty folds,
He poured his loyal Camerons down;
By field and flood they gave their blood
For Charlie Stuart and his crown.
That blood of gentle brave Lochiel
Is throbbing here from head to heel,
As down the loch he laughs and sings,
And cheerly to his strong oar swings.

O generous boy! an earl would give
Broad acres for an heir like thee:
Yea! seldom can they match who live
Of lordly park and pleasaunce free,

The abounding strength, the graceful ease,
Which summer glens and perilous seas
In thee have blended, face and form,—
The sunshine woven with the storm.

The loch is cleared, our day is done,—
Day that will long survive in heart,—
Down the Atlantic slopes the sun,
Meet hour, with such as thee to part:
The sunset heavens, the gleaming seas,
The far transfigured Hebrides,
Break on us round yon headland hoar;
We wave farewell, and meet no more.

THE LASS OF LOCH LINNE.

The spray may drive, the rain may pour,
  Knee-deep in brine, what careth she?
Her brother's boat she'll drag to shore,
  Aloud she'll sing her Highland glee.

Her feet and head alike all bare,
  A drenched plaid swathed about her form,
Around her floats the Highland air,
  Within the Highland blood beats warm.

All night they've toiled and not in vain:
  To count and store the fish be thine;
Then drench thy clothes in morning rain,
  And dry them in the noon sunshine!

The gleam breaks through, the day will clear,
  Then to the peats up yonder glen;
O there is life and freedom here!
  That cannot breathe 'mid throngs of men.

What has thy life and history been?
  Brave lass upon this wind-beat shore!
I may not guess—at distance seen,
  A nameless image, and no more.

Sweet chime the sea beside thy home,
  Thy fire blink bright on heartsome meal!
No more of dearth or clearance come
  To darken down thine own Lochiel!

LOCH FYNE.

Of all the Lochs the Highlands hold,
  Or inland lake or arm of sea,
To the morning sun hath none unrolled
  A bosom full and fair like thee.
Others are flanked by mountain forms
More grandly, raked by wilder storms,
Or welcome more what glory streams
From evening and the western gleams;
But morning and the young sunshine
Thou dost inherit, fair Loch Fyne!

*   *   *   *   *

*   *   *   *   *

THE FOREST OF SLI'-GAOIL.

THAT IS, THE HILL OF LOVE.

In this bare treeless forest lone,
By winds Atlantic overblown,
I sit and hear the weird wind pass
Drearily through the long bent-grass;
And think how that low sighing heard
By Ossian, when no wind was stirred,
Filled his old sightless eyes with tears,
His soul with thoughts of other years,
For the spirits of the men he mourned
In that low eerie sound returned.

And doth not this bleak forest ground
Live in old epic song renowned?
Of him the chief who came of yore
To hunting of the mighty boar,
And left the deed, to float along
The dateless stream of Highland song,
A maid's lorn love, a chief's death-toil,
Still speaking in thy name, Sli'-gaoil!

Well now may harp of Ossian moan,
Through long bent-grass and worn grey stone:
But how could song so long ago,
Come loaded with still elder wo?
Were then, as now, these hills o'ercast
With shadows of some long-gone past?
Did winds, that wandered o'er them, chime
Melodies of a lorn foretime?
As now, the very mountain burns
For something sigh that not returns?

RETURN TO NATURE.

On the braes around Glenfinnan
Fast the human homes are thinning,
And the wilderness is winning
        To itself these graves again.
Names or dates here no man knoweth,
O'er grey headstones heather groweth,
Up Loch-Shiel the sea-wind bloweth
    Over sleep of nameless men.

Who were those forgotten sleepers?
Herdsmen strong, fleet forest-keepers,
Aged men, or widowed weepers
    For their foray-fallen ones?
Babes cut off 'mid childhood's prattle,
Men who lived with herds and cattle,
Clansmen from Culloden battle,
    Camerons, or Clandonald's sons?

Blow ye winds, and rains effacing!
Blur the words of love's fond tracing!
Nature to herself embracing
    All that human hearts would keep:

What they knew of good or evil
Faded, like the dim primeval
Day that saw the vast upheaval
  Of these hills that hold their sleep.

GOAT-MILKING.

When I was a lassie, I raise and was ready,
 In the grey of the dawn o'er Loch Lubnaig to hold,
And up the dark flanks of morn-smitten Benledi,
 Would call my loved milking goats down to the fold.

From high airy peak, and from dark-shadowed corrie,
 The ledge of the crag, and the cleft of the rock,
Weel kenned they my cry, and descending would hurry,
 The grey-bearded sires and the dams of the flock.

To soothe them at milking time, wild strains of Oran
 And Ossian I chaunted, or some bonnie sang
Of bard Duncan-bàn, and his dauted Bendoran,
 Till the crags far and near wi' the melody rang.

But the milking's a' dune, high and low, through the Hielans,
 The hills of the wild goats now ken them no more;
Hands that milked them are cauld, and the bonny blithe shealings
 Are bourocks o' stanes, wi' rank nettles grown o'er.

The auld life is gone, root and branch ; Saxon strangers
Hold a' the hill hirsels we ance ca'd our ain,
And the dun herds of deer, and the few forest-rangers
On the Gael's noblest mountains are all that remain.

Brave hearts now are naught, gold is chieftain and master,
What room in the land for puir bodies like me !
It's time I were safe beyond dool and disaster,
Wi' the lave o' my clan 'neath the auld rowan tree.

CAILLEACH BEIN-Y-VREICH.

WEIRD wife of Bein-y-Vreich! horo! horo!
Aloft in the mist she dwells;
Vreich horo! Vreich horo! Vreich horo!
All alone by the lofty wells.

Weird, weird, wife! with the long grey locks,
She follows her fleet-foot stags,
Noisily moving through splintered rocks,
And crashing the grisly crags.

Tall wife! with the long grey hose, in haste
The rough stony beach she walks;
But dulse or seaweed she will not taste,
Nor yet the green kail stalks.

And I will not let my herds of deer,
My bonny red deer go down;
I will not let them down to the shore,
To feed on the sea-shells brown.

O better they love in the corrie's recess,
Or on mountain top to dwell,

And feed by my side on the green green cress,
  That grows by the lofty well.

Broad Bein-y-Vreich is grisly and drear,
  But wherever my feet have been,
The well-springs start for my darling deer,
  And the grass grows tender and green.

And there high up on the calm nights clear,
  Beside the lofty spring,
They come to my call, and I milk them there,
  And a weird wild song I sing.

But when hunter men round my dun deer prowl,
  I will not let them nigh;
Through the rended cloud I cast one scowl,
  They faint on the heath and die.

And when the north wind o'er the desert bare
  Drives loud, to the corries below
I drive my herds down, and bield them there
  From the drifts of the blinding snow.

Then I mount the blast, and we ride full fast,
  And laugh as we stride the storm,
I, and the witch of the Cruachan Ben,
  And the scowling-eyed Seul-Gorm.

FRAGMENT FROM THE GAELIC.

From the hill that is highest I gaze to discover
On the dim western ocean the boat of my lover:
Wilt thou come to-day? wilt thou come to-morrow?
If thou come not at all, mine is hopeless sorrow.

Ah! oft they are saying, my friends, I must sever
The image of thee from remembrance forever,
As well might they bid the instreaming motion
Of the full-flowing tide to turn back on the ocean.

I gave thee my whole heart, I seek no concealing,
Love, not of a month, nor a year's fitful feeling,
But love that began, when all life was before me,
And love that will last till the grave closes o'er me.

Henceforth shall my life be sad and sick-hearted,
Like the white wounded swan, when the rest all have
parted,
And left her alone, sore-stricken, wing-broken,
To sing her death-wail on the lone grassy lochan.

URRARD.

27th July.

On just such an evening down long Garry stream,
Two centuries gone, fell the sun's setting gleam,
That saw from this braeside the wild battle roll,
And bear from the earth Scotland's gallantest soul.

Long poised on Craighallaig, like earns on their eyry,
They waited—Clanranald, Lochiel, and Glengarry—
Till the sun touched yon hills, and Dundee gave the
word,
And himself to the van on his black charger spurred.

Down the hill-side they plunge, like swoln torrents
descending,
Broom and birch 'neath their headlong tramp crashing
and rending,
And casting their plaids by the fail dykes of Urrard,
Rush claymore and war-axe resistlessly forward.

See the Gael, 'mid the red ranks!—from helmet to heel,
They are cleaving them down with their merciless steel,

Till far through yon dark pass, all jagged and riven,
Roars the flight and the carnage confusedly driven.

Stay, stay, ye wild Athole men, cease your pursuing!
What boots now to drive your foes headlong to ruin?
Here stretched on yon knoll, 'gainst the red setting day,
The life that ye lived by, ebbs fleetly away.

Ah! just in the moment when victory crowned him,
Rang out from yon casement the death-shot that found him;
Yet leal to the last, faltered gallant Dundee,
'If it's well with the King, little matters for me.'

In a plaid wrap him round, bear him quickly to Blair,
Lay him down, let him rest, neath the lowly kirk there;
His wild work is over, God wills there shall shine
O'er the vext hills of Scotland a day more benign.

But whenever ye reckon the count of his guilt,
The innocent blood by his reckless sword spilt,
Remember that last word which flashed out the whole
Life-aim that o'ermastered his chivalrous soul.

A DREAM OF GLEN-SALLACH.

THAT summer glen is far away,
  Who loved me then, their graves are green,
But still that dell and distant day,
  Lie bright in memory's softest sheen.

Are these still there, outspread in space,
  The grey messed-trees, the mountain stream?
Or in some ante-natal place,
  That only cometh back in dream?

There first upon my soul was cast
  Dim reverence, blent with glorious thrills,
From out an old heroic past,
  Lapped in the older calm of hills.

Still after thirty summers loom
  On dreaming hours the lichened trees,
The ivied walls, the warrior's tomb,.
  'Mid those old mountain sanctities.

How awed I stood! where once had kneeled
  The pilgrims by the holy well,

O'er which through centuries unrepealed,
Rome's consecration still doth dwell.

How crept among the broken piles!
And clansmen's grave-stones moss-o'ergrown,
Where rests the Lord of all the Isles,
With plaid and claymore graven in stone.

In deep of noon, mysterious dread
Fell on me in that glimmering glen,
Till, as from haunted ground, I fled
Back to the kindly homes of men.

Thanks to that glen! its scenery blends
With childhood's most ideal hour,
When Highland hills I made my friends,
First owned their beauty, felt their power.

Still, doubtless, o'er Kilbrannan Sound,
As lovely lights from Arran gleam,
'Mid hills that gird Glen Sallach round,
As happy children dream their dream.

The western sea, as deep of tone,
Is murmuring 'gainst that caverned shore;
But, one whole generation gone,
No more those haunts are ours, no more.

DESOLATION.

By the wee birchen corries lie patches of green,
Where gardens and bareheaded bairnies have been,
But the huts now are rickles of stones nettle-grown,
And the once human homes, even their names are
unknown.

But the names that this side the Atlantic have perished,
'Mid far western forests still dearly are cherished,
There men talk of each spot, on the hills that surround
Their long vanished dwellings, as paradise ground.

Not a pass in these hills, not a cairn, nor a corrie.
But lives by the log-fire in legend and story;
And darkly the cloud on their countenance gathers,
As they think on those desolate homes of their
fathers.

O hearts, to the hills of old memory true!
In the land of your love there are mourners for you,
As they wander by peopleless lochside and glen,
Where the red deer are feeding o'er homesteads of
men.

For the stillness they feel o'er the wilderness spread
Is not nature's own silence, but that of the dead;
Even the lone piping plover, and small corrie burn
Seem sighing for those that will never return.

CHANGE.

O MIGHTY mountain pass! from eldest time
  Organ of tempest-breath, and roar of river,
And can it be thy heritage sublime
  Is forfeit now for ever?

Shall all that man hath done not once have drowned
  The mountain music that abides in thee?
Save for a moment when thou heardest sound
  The onset of Dundee,

One single hour, and all again was dumb:
  But now o'ercrowing Tummel's loudest fall
And Garry's thunder, hark the Railway come
  Harsh-shrieking over all.

Ah, what down-crashing! fall thy kingly ones,
  Rock-moorèd oaks, and tempest-sughing pine,
And birches, that have gleamed in summer suns,
  Shimmered in white moonshine.

Along these mountains must we never more
  See silver mists unmixed with railway steam?
Nor hear, without the train's intruding roar,
  Pure voice of wind and stream?

FROM THE BORDERS.

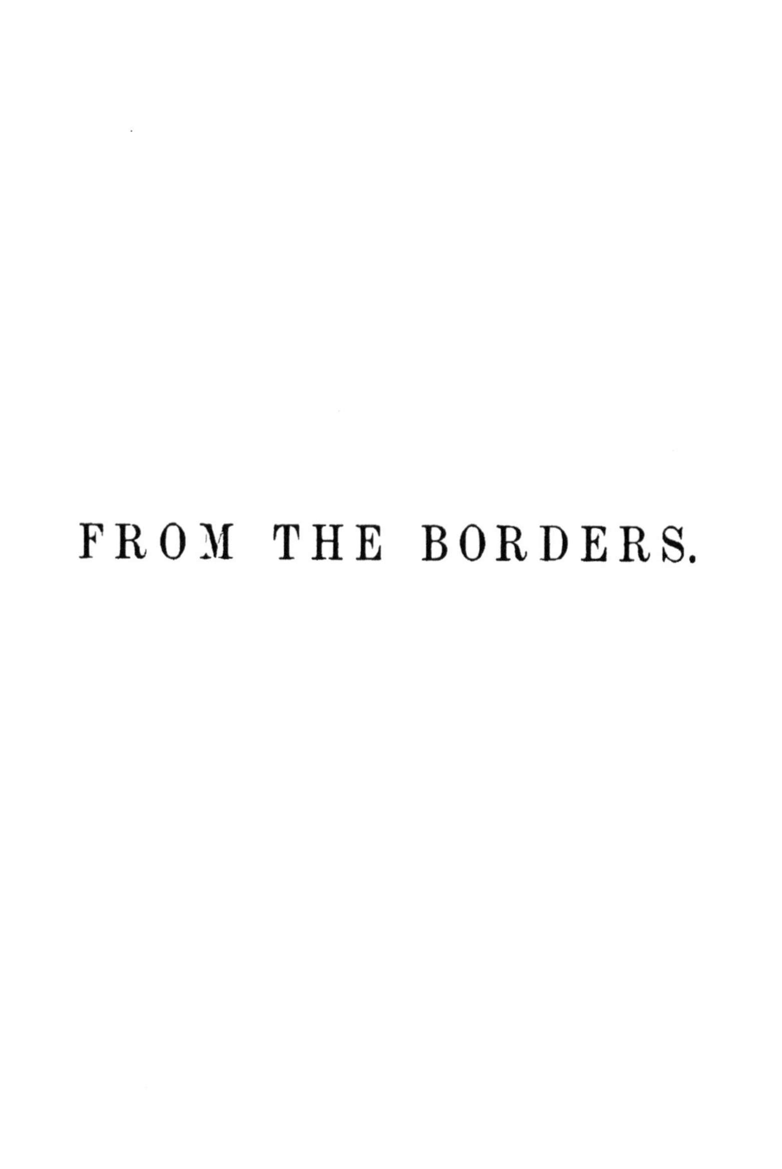

THRIEVE CASTLE.

Whence should ye o'er gentle spirits
 Such o'ermastering power achieve?
Workers of high-handed outrage!
 Making king and people grieve,
O the lawless Lords of Galloway!
 O the bloody towers of Thrieve!

Is it that this time-scarred visage
 From behind five centuries dim,
Doomed to death, yet death-defying,
 Glares the very look of him,
Who first laid these strong foundations,
 Mighty Archibald the Grim?

Impress of those hands is on them,
 That beat Southron foemen down—
Iron hands, that grasped a truncheon
 Weightier than the kingly crown—
Stalwart Earls, broad-browed, black bearded,
 Pinnacled on power o'ergrown.

These were they, lone-thoughted builders
  Of yon grim keep, massy-piled,
Triple-walled, and triple-moated,
  In Dee Island triply isled,
O'er the waste of dun morasses,
  Eyeing Cairnsmore mountains wild.

Power gat pride, pride unforgiveness—
  Whoso crossed the moats of Thrieve,
Captive serf, or lordly foeman,
  Though a monarch begged reprieve,
Had they wronged the Lord of Douglas,
  Living ne'er these gates might leave.

Downward! rust in yon dark dungeon
  Rings that once held fettered thrall,
High in air,—the grooved stone gallows
  Ghastly juts from yonder wall,
Where once swung the corse of Bombie,
  Prelude of the Douglas fall.

Never since from thy scathed forehead
  Hath it passed, the bodeful gloom
Gathered there the hour thy haughtiest
  Lord rode forth, defying doom,
To the monarch's perjured poignard,
  And the deathly banquet room.

Outcast now from human uses,
Both by war and peace disowned,
All thy high ambitions broken,
All thy dark deeds unatoned,
Still thou wear'st no meaner aspect,
Than a despot King dethroned.

Frost and rain, and storm and thunder—
Time's strong wedges—let them cleave
Breaches through thy solid gables,
Thou wilt neither blench nor grieve;
Thou who gav'st, wilt ask, no pity,
Unrelenting Castle Thrieve!

DEVORGUILLA:

OR THE ABBEY OF THE SWEET HEART.

In grey Criffel's lap of granite
  Lies the Abbey, saintly fair!
Well the heart, that first did plan it,
  Finds her earthly resting there:

Who from out an age of wildness,
  Lawless force, unbridled crime,
Reachèd forth wise hands in mildness
  Helpful to the coming time.

The rude Galloway chieftain's daughter—
  Memory of her Norman knight,
And long widowed sorrow taught her
  To make good deeds her delight.

Long ere now their names had perished,
  Had not those wise halls, she reared
By the southern Isis, cherished
  Them for Founders' names revered.

While these arches o'er Nith river,
  Thronged by daily passers, still
Witness here her pure endeavour
  To complete her dear lord's will.

But for human use or learning
  Good works done, could they appease
Her long heartache? that lone yearning
  Other medicine asked than these.

So she spake, 'Rise, page, and ride in
  Haste, this grief will not be calmed,
Till thou from the land he died in
  Bear my dead lord's heart embalmed.'

Ivory casket closing round it,
  With enamelled silver, fair
As deft hands could frame, he bound it,
  And with fleet hoofs homeward bare:

Generous heart that once so truly
  With young love for her had beat,
Bore he to her home, and duly
  Laid before the lady's feet.

One whole day her passionate sorrow
  Inly brooded, dark and dumb,
But in silence shaped, the morrow
  Clear as light her words did come.

"Build me here, high-towered and solemn,
Abbey-church in fairest style,—
Pointed arch, and fluted column,
Ranged down transept, nave, and aisle."

There the dear heart laid in holy
Place, the altar-steps before,
Down she knelt herself in lowly
Adoration on that floor.

Thither day by day she wended,
On that same spot knelt and prayed;
There at last, when all was ended,
With the heart she loved was laid.

In that place of ivied ruin
She hath taken, since the close
Of her life of full well-doing,
Six long centuries' repose.

Meek one! who, 'mid proud men violent,
A pure builder unreproved,
Lived and laboured for the silent
Kingdom that shall ne'er be moved.

THE LAST OF THE FOREST.

Ash-trees, gnarled, bent, and hoary!
Whence have they this marvellous power?
Is the whole forest's perished glory
Resting on them for a dower?

Foray rides and battle riot,
That adown this vale have driven,
Blend they here with summer quiet
Of these green hills calm as heaven?

Now the thread that had unravelled
All their meaning I had caught,
Now, like thistle-down far travelled,
Cloudward it hath passed from thought.

Painter! come thou here and gather
Wealth of summer's goldenest days;
Catch each tint the changing weather
Traileth o'er these idle braes.

And wouldst thou their secret render,
  Watch these few last lorn ash-trees,
In this hour of braeside splendour,
  With the bracken round their knees:

Stems grey-lichened, green leaves gleaming,
  And yon smooth majestic slope,
With one stray cloud-shadow dreaming
  Upward to its skyey cope.

When thy fairest gleam is given,
  A whole summer's hoarded skill,
Something or of earth or heaven,
  Will I ween be wanting still.

Poet! dowered with natural feeling
  Deep as Wordsworth's, draw thou nigh,
When the hills are most revealing
  Secrets to the gifted eye.

Trancèd there, in sunshine glinting
  Will these trees reveal to thee
All the meanings they are hinting,
  Past. and present, and to be?

Nay! when thou thy best hast chaunted,
  I will here return and feel,
By some unvoiced music haunted,
  Word nor art of man reveal.

THE SHEPHERD LADY.

Lady Anne, she loved the shepherd lad,
And her love, it seemed like madness,
When he was by, her heart was glad,
When away she drooped for sadness.

She followed him high on his mountain gang
A' the gowden simmer days,
And she sat and lilted her sweetest sang
Beside him on the braes.

Ae nicht when nor' winds filled the lift,
Rough words her father spake,
And drave him forth to the blinding drift,
Though her heart was like to break.

She followed far on his eerie track,
And sought him frae morn till even,
Neist day she fand him stretched on his back
Wi' his blae cauld face to heaven.

She fand him lying stiff and stark
On the windy side o' the hill,
And she carried him hame through the nicht so dark,
And the snell winds freezing chill.

And she waked him weary days and nights,
Till the drifts frae the hills were gane,
Syne bore him up to the heathery heights,
And buried him all her lane.

Then she left her father's castle, and made
Her hame 'neath the flinty rock,
With her lover's staff and his shepherd's plaid,
To watch his bonny flock.

Nae mair she spake to living men,
Nor human hame cam' near;
But she sang to the sheep a woe-wild strain,
When nane were by to hear.

She wandered wide over muir and dale;
I wot they were great ferliè,
The bonny flock and the lady pale,
Through a' the south countrie.

The farm-folk brought her milk and bread,
As she moved on the hills aloof;
But still the muirland bare was her bed,
And the starry heaven her roof.

And ilka time she passed each place,
  Her flock were worn mair few,
And ilka time seemed the lady's face
  Mair crined and wan of hue.

And mony a year is gane sin' last
  She and her flock were seen,
But nane can tell when frae earth she passed,
  Nor where her grave is green.

RENWICK.

You see yon burn that from the mountain cleuch
Comes pouring, follow it through the folding hills
'Twill guide you to a nook, none lonelier lies
Between the Yarrow and Ettrick. One grey thorn,
The sole survivor of the old forest thorns,
Stands single there—no other tree in sight,—
Fronting the meeting of two mountain burns,
The main burn and a sister. Other thorns.
As goodly, may be goodlier to the eye,
Still live, each spring rekindling into green,
By cleuchs or hopes among the Border hills;
But this tree hath a story of its own,
That more endears it than the famous thorn
By Douglas burn, once sung by Walter Scott.
And since his day quite vanished.

Hither came,—
In those dark times when Scotland's noblest souls,
To keep clean conscience, and a worship pure,
Flying from Galloway and all the west,
Last refuge found by Whitecoomb and Loch Skene,
From Clavers and his troopers—hither came
Renwick with soul of fire, and round him flocked

From all their hiding dens, and caves of the earth,
By Moffat water and the dusky moors,
And black moss hags of Chapelhope and Loch Skene,
The hunted remnant of the Covenant,
True men and women with their souls athirst
For God, the living God. In this green place.
Upon the braeside by that aged thorn
They met, and sang to Him their soul-like psalm.
That ended, Renwick's voice alone arose,
Cleaving the heavens with prayer, while round him stood
Grey-headed elders leaning on broadswords,
And women with wan faces bowed to earth.
This hour entranced on the adoring heights,
The next, to be plunged down to murderous death.
There by that thorn tree the young preacher stood.
And to the flock between him and the burn
Spoke out his last strong message from the Lord.
What were the words he spake? The men who heard,
They bore them in their hearts down to the grave,
And these green hills, their echoes heard them too.
But tell them not again. Yet I not doubt,
That old men drinking the soul-piercing words,
And gazing on the fair rapt countenance
With spiritual fire transfigured, and the hair,
Long golden hair, gleaming down all his back,
Grew strong to suffer and to die with him,
So young and yet so valiant for the Lord.

And last, upon that strip of sward he stood,
Where the two waters meet, and muirmen bore
Down to the brink their little ones in their arms.
There Renwick laid on them strong holy vows,
And with pure water lifted from the burn
Sprinkled the faces of the innocents,
And o'er them breathing the thrice holy name
Commended them and all that company
To the Lord their God for ever.
                                        Then he passed
Far hence, by the Spirit, like Elijah, borne,
And they who heard him here beheld no more
His face on earth. When next they heard of him,
His limbs were swinging from the gallows-tree,
Under the Edinborough castle rock,
Youngest and last of Scotland's martyr sons.

BLACKHOPE GRAIN.

DARK is the hollow, with black rocks in-walled,
And yet it keeps one mound of tenderest green;
The cauldron sides are rifted, and storm-scrawled.
That spot is all serene:

The sunbeams touch it lovingly—well they may;
In this gorge—haply on yon very mound—
Sons of the Covenant in their evil day
Brief rest for worship found.

And all this desert blossoms with the flower
Of their good memories,—green for ever be,
And holy these hills for one hallowing hour
Out of a blank eternity.

O WILLIE EAST.

O Willie east and Willie wast,
And Willie's unco bonny,
And Willie's hecht to marry me,
Gin e'er he marry ony.

O Willie Laidlaw's the wale o' men,
A trusty and a true heart,
And aye he's welcome up the glen,
Whar wons his Mary Stuart.

And whether blaws the mountain thyme,
Or blooms the purple heather,
The ae sweet hour 's the faulding time,
When he and I forgather.

He bughts for me the milkin' ewes,
He stands aside me singing,
Syne bears my bowie ower the knowes,
His plaidie round me flinging.

O sweet to kirk on Sabbath calm,
  Ower the hills wi' him to wander,
And sweet to sing the evening psalm,
  Doun in our wee cot yonder.

O Willie east and Willie wast,
  And Willie's gude as bonny,
And either I'll be Willie's wife,
  Or ne'er be wife to ony.

THE MOORS.

O THE moors! the moors! the purple moors!
It's pleasant there to be,
O'er lowne green dell, and breezy fell.
In day-long wandering free.

Ay! wandering there with forehead bare.
To meet the westlin' wind,
Coming up thro' the dells o' the heather bells,
Frae the sea it has left behind.

To daunder wide, or on green hillside
To lie, nor count the time,
At ease to croon some auld warld tune,
And weave a sister rhyme;

While autumn showers skiff o'er the moors,
And blinks o' sunny sheen
On the purple tint of the heather glint,
Or the bright green sward between.

There scream of wheeling whaup by fits
From far and near is borne,
On mossy flowe the plover sits,
And pipes her note forlorn.

The Covenanter's grave is there,
With wild thyme overgrown,
And hallowed still are muir and hill
For that memorial stone.

There evermore, ye bees! hum o'er
The peasant martyr's grave,
Thy wail be heard, lone plover bird!
O'er Scotland's holy brave.

THE BUSH ABOON TRAQUAIR.

Will ye gang wi' me and fare
To the bush aboon Traquair?
Owre the high Minchmuir we'll up and awa',
This bonny summer noon,
While the sun shines fair aboon,
And the licht sklents saftly doun on holm and ha'.

And what would ye do there,
At the bush aboon Traquair?
A lang driech road, ye had better let it be;
Save some auld skrunts o' birk
I' the hill-side lirk,
There's nocht i' the warld for man to see.

But the blithe lilt o' that air,
'The Bush aboon Traquair,'
I need nae mair, it's eneuch for me;
Owre my cradle its sweet chime
Cam' sughin' frae auld time,
Sae tide what may, I'll awa' and see.

And what saw ye there
At the bush aboon Traquair?
Or what did ye hear that was worth your heed?
I heard the cushies croon
Through the gowden afternoon,
And the Quair burn singing doun to the Vale o' Tweed.

And birks saw I three or four,
Wi' grey moss bearded owre,
The last that are left o' the birken shaw,
Whar mony a simmer e'en
Fond lovers did convene,
Thae bonny bonny gloamins that are lang awa'.

Frae mony a but and ben,
By muirland, holm, and glen,
They cam' ane hour to spen' on the greenwood sward;
But lang hae lad an' lass
Been lying 'neth the grass,
The green green grass o' Traquair kirkyard.

They were blest beyond compare,
When they held their trysting there,
Amang thae greenest hills shone on by the sun;
And then they wan a rest,
The lownest and the best,
I' Traquair kirkyard when a' was dune.

Now the birks to dust may rot,
Names o' lnvers be forgot,
Nae lads and lasses there ony mair convene;
But the blithe lilt o' yon air
Keeps the bush aboon Traquair,
And the luve that ance was there, aye fresh and green.

THEN AND NOW.

A TIME there was,
When this hill-pass,
With castle, keep, and peel,
Stood iron-teethed,
Like warrior sheathed
In mail from head to heel.

Friend or foe,
No man might go,
Out to the English Border,
Nor any ride
To Forth or Clyde,
Unchallenged of the Warder.

At the baron's 'hest
The trooper spurred,
And brought the traveller
Before his lord,
To be dungeon-mured,
Dark, damp, and lone,

Till death had cured
His weary moan.

ht time has pulled the teeth
From those fierce fangs,
bread his sward of heath
O'er the riever gangs;
Hushed their castles proud,
As grave-yards still,
And streamed life loud
Through mart and mill.

mbowered among green ashes,
The grey towers sigh, Alas!
s the loud train crashes
Down the rock-ribbed pass.
They come and g
n and eve
riend a
k no

o to
n th
al

Chiefs ruled

Till death had cured
His weary moan.

But time has pulled the teeth
From those fierce fangs,
Spread his sward of heath
O'er the riever gangs;
Hushed their castles proud,
As grave-yards still,
And streamed life loud
Through mart and mill.

Embowered among green ashes.
The grey towers sigh, Alas!
As the loud train crashes
Down the rock-ribbed pass.
They come and go
Morn and eve,
Bear friend and foe,
And ask no leave.

While the towers look forth
From their gaunt decay
On an altered earth,
A strange new day;
When mechanics pale
Oust feudal lords,

With wheel and rail,
Not blood-red swords;
And the horny hands
That delve iron-ore,
Grasp mighty lands,
Chiefs ruled of yore.

THE HAIRST RIG.

O how my heart lap to her
  Upon the blithe hairst rig!
Ilk morning comin' owre the fur
  Sae gracefu', tall, and trig.

Chorus—O the blithe hairst rig!
  The blithe hairst rig;
  Fair fa' the lads and lasses met
  On the blithe hairst rig!

At twal' hours aft we sat aloof,
  Aneth the bielding stook,
And tently frae her bonny loof
  The thistle thorns I took.

When hairst was dune and neebors met
  To haud the canty kirn,
Sae fain we twa to steal awa'
  And daunder up the burn.

The lammies white as new fa'en drift,
  Lay quiet on the hills,

The clouds aboon i' the deep blue lift.
  Lay whiter, purer still.

Ay, pearly white, the clouds that night
  Shone marled to the moon,
But nought like you, my bonny doo!
  All earth or heaven aboon.

The burnie whimpering siller clear,
  It made a pleasant tune;
But O! there murmured in my ear
  A sweeter holier soun'.

Lang lang we cracked, and went and came,
  And daundered, laith to part;
But the ae thing I daured na name
  Was that lay neist my heart.

Fareweel cam' owre and owre again,
  And yet we could na sever,
Till words were spake in that dear glen,
  That made us ane forever.

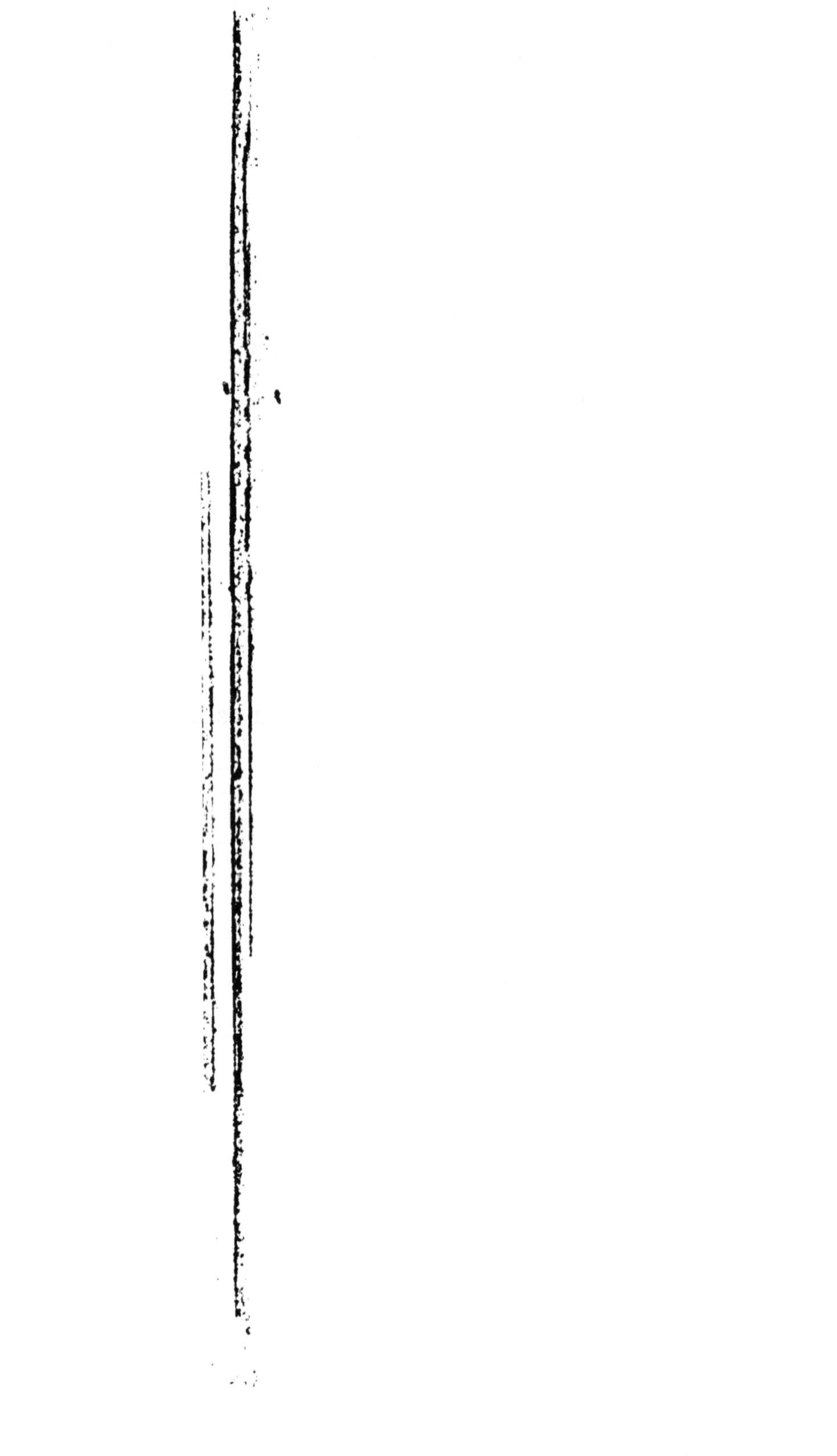

FROM THE LOWLANDS.

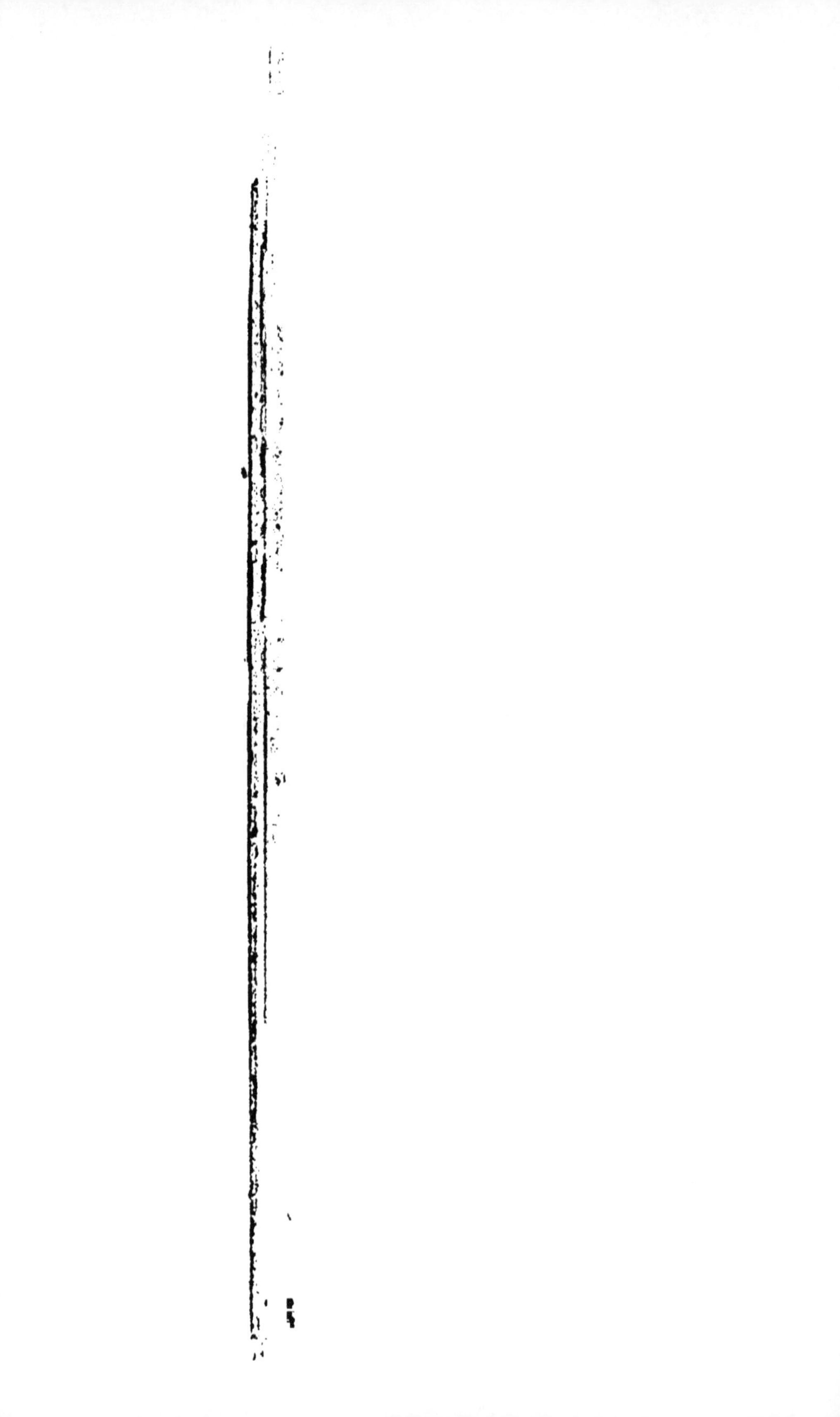

THE BONSPIEL.

Cauld and snell is the weather, ye curlers! come gather,
Scotland summons her best frae the Tweed to the Tay,
It's the North o' the Clyde, 'gainst the Southern side,
And Loch Winnoch the tryst for the bonspiel to-day.

Ilk parish they've summoned, baith landward and
borough,
Far and near troop the lads wi' the stanes and the
broom,
The ploughs o' the Loudons stand stiff i' the furrow,
And the weavers o' Beith for the loch leave the loom.

The braw shepherd lads, they are there in their plaids,
Their hirsels they've left on the Tweedside their lane,
Grey carles frae the moorlands, wi' gleg e'e and sure
hands,
Braid bannet o' blue, and the big channel stane.

And the Loudons three, they forgather in glee
Wi' tounsfolk frae Ayr, and wi' farmers on Doon,
Out over the Forth come the lads frae the North,
Frae the far Athole braes and the palace o' Scone.

Auld Reekie's top sawyers, the lang-headed lawyers,
And crouse Glasgow merchants are loud i' the play,
There are lairds frae the east, there are lords frae the
wast,
For the peer and the ploughman are marrows to-day.

See the rinks are a' marshalled, how cheerly they
mingle!
Blithe callants, stout chiels, and auld grey-headed
men,
And the roar o' their stanes gars the snowy heights
tingle,
As they ne'er did before, and may never again.
Some lie at hog-score, some owre a' ice roar,
'Here's the tee,' 'there's the winner,' 'chap and lift
him twa yards,'
'Lay a guard,' 'fill the port,' and now there's nocht
for't,
But a canny inwick, or a rub at the guards.'

Gloamin' comes, we maun pairt, but fair fa' ilk kind
heart!
Wi' the auld Scottish blood beating warm in his veins,
Curlers! aye we've been leal to our countrie's weal,
Though our swords now are besoms, our targes are
stanes.

We are sons o' the true men who bled wi' Will Wallace.
And conquered at brave Bannockburn wi' the Bruce,
Thae wild days are gane, but their memories call us,
So we'll stand by langsyne and the guid ancient use.

And we'll hie to the spiel, as our fathers afore us,
Ye sons o' the men whom foe never could tame,
And at nicht round the ingle we'll raise the loud chorus
To the land we lo'e weel and our auld Scottish game.

THE RUN.

Hark hollo! brave hearts!
  'Twas the hounds I heard;
With the sound of their going
  All the land is stirred.
They have made every peasant
  From work stand still,
With gazers they've crowned
  Every crag and hill.

And the ploughman cried loud,
  By my team I stood,
And heard them crashing
  Yon old fir wood.
Down yon ash-tree river banks,
  Where the sunbeams slant and fall,
Flashed the dappled hounds,
  Making the dells musical.
For sweeter they be,
  Than any chime of bells,
The melodies that linger
  All year in yon dells,
Till the hounds come by and awake them.

And the pedlar answered,
From beneath his load,
At noon they went streaming
Right o'er my road.
From the farmsteads the lassies
Rushed out to see,
How they skimmed like swallows,
Over plough and lea.
As they went to the hills
What a head they bare !
Like snow-drift scudding
On the stormy air,
And few were the steeds could o'ertake them.

Forward waved the shepherd,
They are west away,
On the moorlands startling
The plover grey.
Ever on as they sped,
More mute they grew,
And the riders waxed fewer,
And yet more few,
Till one only hunter attended.

And the widow, as she sat
On her lone cottage-floor,
Heard their cry thro' the dark
On the midnight moor ;

And at morn came the worn hounds
Home, one by one,
And the huntsman knew
That the chase was done,
Never knew how nor where it ended.

THE LOOSING TIME.

O WALCUM fa's the twal' hours, and sweet the morning prime,
But sweetest hour o' the twenty-four is heartsome loosing time.
When lads a' kythe and lasses blithe, their harvest day's darg done,
Come laughing hame, and daffing hame, fornent the westerin' sun.

Young Jeanie bides na supper, but buskit clean and neat,
She's owre the gleaming moorland, her lover lad to meet.
O what has warle's wealth to gi'e! like the full heart's raptured chime,
That gloamin' hour i' the bracken glen, 'yont blithesome loosing time.

Then pleased the bandster sees his lum i' the gowden sunset reek,
And his bairnies round the gavel for their daddie wait and keek,

Sae kind's they claught his haffit locks, his knees sae fondly climb,
And his wife sae clean mak's a' sae bien 'gainst walcum loosing time.

The auld carle i' the sheugh, a' day forfoughten sair,
Weet and draigled, daunders hame to his kimmer and arm-chair,
Though she be frail wi' pains, and his pow like frosty rime,
Yet fain the twa auld bodies meet at easefu' loosing time.
Haud up, auld hearts! the moil and toil will a' be ended sune,
Ye've had a weary warsle here, but your reward's aboon,
He'll bring, gin ye but lippen Him, a better Loosing time,
When ye'll be by wi' a' the toil o' this wark-weary clime.

THE BLUE BELLS.

AGAIN the bonny blue bêlls
  Wave all o'er our dear land,
Or scattered single, here and there,
  Or a numerous sister band.

How many a last leave-taking
  Hath darkened over youthful faces,
Since the hour ye last were here!
  Now in all your wonted places,
From long wintry sleep awaking,
  Blithe ye reappear.

The same ye meet us, be we joyful,
  Or bowed down by heavy loads,
On the thatch of auld clay biggins,
  Shedding grace o'er poor abodes,
Or from dykes of greensward gleaming,
  Hard by unfrequented roads.

O'er the linns of dark Clyde water
  Ye are trembling, from the steep,

And afar on dusky moorlands,
Where the shepherd wears his sheep,
By the hoary headstone waving
O'er the Covenanter's sleep.

Ye come ere laverocks cease their singing,
And abide through sun and rain,
Till our harvest-homes are ended,
And the barn-yards stored with grain;
Then ye pass, when flock the plover
To warm lands beyond the main.

In your old haunts, O happy blue bells!
Ye, when we are gone, shall wave,
And as living we have loved you,
Dead, one service would we crave,
Come, and in the west winds swinging,
Prank the sward that folds our grave.

WEAVING.

At morn I saw them weaving
  To a pleasant tune,
But I knew the rending and the grieving
  Would come ere afternoon.

The tints were fair and spangled,
  And they wove with guileless art,
But every thread they tangled
  Was dipt in hues of heart.

Happy dreamful singers!
  Lilting at the loom,
Broidering in with eager fingers
  Flowers of rarest bloom.

Blue the sea before them,
Far the mountains blue,
But behind stern destiny o'er them
Dark her shadow threw.

Alas! when all is ended,
And they are doomed to part,
And every thread that's rended
Is the fibre of a heart.

THE TEMPLARS' TOWER.

And did these bare walls once witness
  Templar Knights of wide renown,
Loose their brands, unbar their vizors,
  Seat them to high banquets down?

Have these worm-grooved oaken rafters,
  Dust-begrimed and cobweb-spread,
Shaken to heroic laughters,
  Echoed back the armèd tread?

Carved jambs gape with wide hearth-places,
  Where long-since extinguished fires
Lit broad brows and sun-browned faces,
  From far lands, of famous sires.

When from this quaint tower the foemen
  Loomed afar, these hurried down,

Sprang to horse, withstood their coming
 In the gate of this old town.

Woe is me, for tower and chamber!
 Fallen now to uses vile,
Walls, where bat and spider clamber,
 Floors, which loathly sights defile.

LOST AND FOUND.

When the Eighty-eight, brave Connaught rangers,
On the gory steeps of Inkermann,
Forward dashed through thickest deaths and dangers,
Broken, foe-encompassed, rear and van.

One poor lad from western Connemara,
Sundered wide from his compatriot ranks,
Gazing round a moment, heard afar a
Bugle blowing onset of the Franks.

Thither flying found he welcome sheltering,
One red stranger with blue Zouaves blent,
Charged and charged the Russian columns, weltering
All day long upon that sheer ascent;

Swelled the Gallic shout with British cheering,
Spake, but none there understood his tongue,
Till one kindly voice said in his hearing
Words that to his inmost bosom rung.

Can it be? and yet it is no other,
None but his tongue hath that dear home-sound,

Yes, it is my only, long lost brother,
Long despaired of, now in battle found.

Many a day barefoot they trod the heather,
Children wont all joys and griefs to halve,
Now they charge and win the field together,
Connaught Ranger with the brave Zouave.

LETTER FROM BALAKLAVA.

THE NIGHT AFTER THE CHARGE.

At morn three comrades in one tent,
  We laughed to hear the bugles blown,
On saddle sprung, and forward went—
  To-night I sit alone.

All three abreast through blinding smoke
  We dashed into the deadly vale,
On front and flank the cannon broke,
  But no heart there did quail.

We trode them down, those squadrons proud,
  Charged the red fire of their redoubt,
Three side by side, we pierced that cloud,
  But only one rode out.

I did not see them dashed to dust,
  Saw but their chargers break away;
A thousand hoofs came on—they must
  Have trampled them to clay.

But forward like a tempest wind
  Swept on our charge, till all was clear,
Then wildly arose that cry behind,
  "They are closing round our rear!"

Our chief was gone—I gave command,
  'Wheel,' 'backward charge,' and on we drove,
The skeleton of our noble band
  Right through that army clove.

My charger, bathed in blood and foam,
  His shoulder broken, rended side,
The gallant beast, he bore me home
  Dying every stride.

That frantic ride! the world wide
  May ring aloud with its renown,
But mother and bride will rue that ride,
  Their darlings there went down.

PRAYER.

Ye tell us prayer is vain—that the divine plan
Disowns it, and as waves in-driven from mid-seas
Break on the headlands, Nature's strong decrees
Dash back his weakness on the heart of man.
Against the universe who can prevail?
Will a voice cleave the everlasting bars?
The heart's poor sigh o'er-soar the loftiest stars,
And through all laws to a Divine Will scale?
Too oft will the perplexed soul question thus,
And yet these great laws that encompass us
Of the meanest things on earth consult the weal,
Are very pitiful to the worms and weeds.
Turn they a deaf ear when the warm heart pleads?
He who did plant that heart, will He not feel?

RELIEF.

Who seeketh finds: what shall be his relief
Who hath no power to seek, no heart to pray,
No sense of God, but bears as best he may,
A lonely incommunicable grief?
What shall he do? One only thing he knows,
That his life flits a frail uneasy spark
In the great vast of universal dark,
And that the grave may not be all repose.
Be still, sad soul! lift thou no passionate cry,
But spread the desert of thy being bare
To the full searching of the All-seeing eye:
Wait—and through dark misgiving, blank despair,
God will come down in pity, and fill the dry
Dead place with light, and life, and vernal air.

GRASMERE.

SINCE our long summer in yon blissful nook,
Six years, not changeless, intervene;
Those friends all scattered, I return and look
Down on this peace serene.

O happy vision! depth of spirit-balm!
For hearts that have too deeply yearned,
This still lake holding his majestic calm
'Mid his green hills inurned.

There dwell, repeated the clear depths among,
Hills more aerial, skies of fairyer cloud,
Hard by, yon homestead, where the summer long
Our laughters once were loud.

Still gleam the birch-trees down that pass as fair,
Nor less melodious breaks
The Rotha murmuring down his rocky lair,
Between his sister lakes.

PARTING.

O DOOMED to go to sunnier climes,
  With the wa'-gang o' the swallow,
Thee prayers, far-borne from happier times
  And earnest friendship, follow.

Thou leav'st us, ere from moorlands wild
  The plover-flocks have flown,
For lands that have their winters mild,
  As summer in thine own.

Sadly we watch that vessel's track
  O'er the wan autumnal sea,
For spring that brings the swallow back
  Will bring no word of thee.

Thy 'wound is deep,' earth's balmiest breeze
  Can breathe no healing now :

Those eyes must close on lands and seas,
  To ope, ah! where, and how?

O breathe on him, thou better breath!
  That can the soul-sick heal,
And as the mortal languisheth,
  The immortal life reveal.

ON HEARING OF SIR W. R. GILBERT'S DEATH,

JUST AFTER HE LANDED IN ENGLAND.

He came from well-fought Indian fields,
His brows all blanched and hoary,
To claim whate'er, his country yields
Her conquering sons, of glory.

God had for him another call,
To which is no replying,
Not to proud place in Senate hall,
But to lone bed of dying.

Earth's triumphs then his soul forsook,
Like friends found false and hollow,
And memory bad no backward look
For Sobraon or Chillian-wallah.

The dashing charge he heedeth not,
His heart reverteth solely
To that plain word his mother taught,—
Christ died for the unholy!

O! lay him in the churchyard grave,
With those who first did love him,
No banner—but for ever wave
His native yews above him!

POETIC TRUTH.

O for truth-breathèd music! soul-like lays!
Not of vain-glory born, nor love of praise,
But welling purely from profound heart-springs,
That lie deep down amid the life of things,
And singing on, heedless though mortal ear
Should never their lone murmur overhear.

When through the world shall voice of poet shine,
Alike true to the human and divine?
Full of the heart of man, yet fuller fed
At the o'erflow of that divine well-head,
From which, as tiny drops, to earth is brought
Whate'er is pure of love, and true in thought,
To which all spirits, in the flesh that be,
Are as scant rillets to the infinite sea.

MEMORIES.

As the far seen peaks of Alpine ranges
In their robe of virgin snow endure,
High o'er Europe plains and earthborn changes,
Calmly and imperishably pure.

Thus, e'en thus, so lofty and so holy,
O'er our poor life's ordinary moods
High aloof, yet very loving and lowly,
Shine the blessèd Christ's Beatitudes.

Near them Paul's pure charity eternal
Dwelling keeps, above earth's cloudy clime,
Beckoning worn hearts upward by its vernal
Brightness from these murky flats of time.

And from off those summits do not voices,
All divine, yet very human, come?
Hearing which awe-struck the soul rejoices,
As at echoes from a long-lost home.

Deem not these are young earth's hymeneal
   Chaunts, no after age can ere repeat;
Something all at variance with the real
   World that meets us in the field and street.

Doth not memory from the past recover
   Some who near us once did move and breathe,
Names, that as we read those high words over,
   Fitly might be written underneath?

Blessèd gifts of God, that our poor weakness
   Might not only hear, but soothly see,
What of truth and love, what might of meekness,
   In our flesh in very deed might be.

While they here sojourned their presence drew us
   By the sweetness of their human love,
Day by day good thoughts of them renew us,
   Like fresh tidings from the world above;

Coming, like the stars at gloamin' glinting
   Through the western clouds, when loud winds cease,
Silently of that calm country hinting,
   Where they with the angels are at peace.

Not their own, ah! not from earth was flowing
   That high strain to which their souls were tuned,
Year by year we saw them inly growing
   Liker Him with whom their hearts communed.

Then to Him they passed; but still unbroken,
Age to age, lasts on that goodly line,
Whose pure lives are, more than all words spoken,
Earth's best witness to the life divine.

Subtlest thought shall fail, and learning falter,
Churches change, forms perish, systems go,
But our human needs, they will not alter,
Christ no after age shall ere outgrow.

Yea, amen! O changeless One, Thou only
Art life's guide and spiritual goal,
Thou the Light across the dark vale lonely,—
Thou the eternal haven of the soul!

HIDDEN LIFE.

Ay, true it is, our dearest, best beloved,
Of us unknowing, are by us unknown,
That from our outward survey far removed,
Deep down they dwell, unfathomed and alone.

We gaze on their loved faces, hear their speech,
The heart's most earnest utterance,—yet we feel
Something beyond, nor they nor we can reach,
Something they never can on earth reveal.

Dearly they loved us, we returned our best,
They passed from earth, and we divined them not,
As though the centre of each human breast
Were a sealed chamber of unuttered thought.

Hidden from others do we know ourselves?
Albeit the surface takes the common light;
Who hath not felt that this our being shelves
Down to abysses, dark and infinite?

As to the sunlight some basaltic isle
  Upheaves a scanty plain, far out from shore,
But downward plungeth sheer walls many a mile,
  'Neath the unsunned ocean floor.

So some small light of consciousness doth play
  On the surface of our being, but the broad
And permanent foundations every way
  Pass into mystery, are hid in God.

The last outgoings of our wills are ours;
  What moulded them, and fashioned down below,
And gave the bias to our nascent powers,
  We cannot grasp nor know.

O Thou on whom our blind foundations lean,
  In whose hand our wills' primal fountains be,
We cannot—but Thou canst—O make them clean!
  We cast ourselves on Thee.

From the foundations of our being breathe
  Up all their darkened pores pure light of thine,
Till, in that light transfigured from beneath,
  We in Thy countenance shine.

EDINBURGH: T. CONSTABLE.
PRINTER TO THE QUEEN, AND TO THE UNIVERSITY

Lightning Source UK Ltd.
Milton Keynes UK
UKHW020906230119
336059UK00010B/529/P